Study Guide for the Praxis *Education of Young Children Tests*

▶ ▶ ▶ ▶ ▶ ▶ ▶ ▶ ▶ ▶ ▶ ▶ ▶

A PUBLICATION OF EDUCATIONAL TESTING SERVICE

Table of Contents
Study Guide for the Praxis
Education of Young Children Tests

► ► ► ► ► ► ► ► ► ► ►

Chapter 1

Introduction to the Praxis *Education of Young Children* Tests and Suggestions for Using This Study Guide

▶   ▶   ▶   ▶   ▶   ▶   ▶   ▶   ▶   ▶   ▶   ▶

Introduction to the Three Praxis *Education of Young Children* Tests

This study guide covers three Praxis tests that assess understanding of key concepts that teachers of young children need to know to do their jobs: *Early Childhood Education* (0020), *Education of Young Children* (0021), and *Pre-Kindergarten Education* (0530). These tests are based on a teaching approach that emphasizes the active involvement of young children in a variety of play and child-centered activities that provide opportunities for choices, decision making, and discovery.

In developing assessment material for these tests, ETS (Educational Testing Service) has worked in collaboration with educators, higher-education content specialists, and accomplished practicing teachers to keep the tests updated and representative of current standards. The *Education of Young Children* (0021) test also was designed to align with the National Association for the Education of Young Children's *NAEYC Standards for Early Childhood Professional Preparation* (2001).

The *Early Childhood Education* (0020) Test

The Praxis *Early Childhood Education* (0020) test consists of 120 multiple-choice questions. The test assesses your knowledge of the growth, development, and learning of young children and your understanding of the primary factors that influence children's development and learning. A number of questions are devoted to appropriate teaching applications of this knowledge and understanding, and others focus on curriculum planning, evaluation and reportings of student progress, and the professional and legal responsibilities of teachers of young children. Although most questions refer to children ages 3 through 8, a few questions concern development at earlier and later ages to examine the full range of early childhood development.

The test covers six major categories of content:

Content Categories	Approximate Number of Questions	Approximate Percentage of Examination
I. The Growth, Development, and Learning of Young Children	37	31%
II. Factors Influencing Individual Growth and Development	12	10%
III. Applications of Developmental and Curriculum Theory	14	12%
IV. Planning and Implementing Curriculum	35	29%
V. Evaluating and Reporting Student Progress and the Effectiveness of Instruction	15	12%
VI. Understanding Professional and Legal Responsibilities	7	6%

You have two hours to complete the test.

The *Education of Young Children* (0021) Test

The Praxis *Education of Young Children* (0021) test has two parts. Part A consists of 60 multiple-choice questions; Part B consists of six short constructed-response questions. You answer constructed-response questions by writing out your response. It is not accurate to call a constructed-response question an essay question, since your response will not be graded on the basis of how it succeeds as an essay. Instead, your constructed response will be graded on the basis of how well it demonstrates an understanding of the principles of education and their appropriate application.

Most of the multiple-choice and short constructed-response questions are related to children ages 3 through 8, but some questions may require knowledge of development at earlier and later ages in order to assess your understanding of the full developmental range found among children in early-childhood education settings. Each of the six constructed-response questions focuses on one of the following areas: the learning environment, working with families, instruction, assessment, professionalism, and diversity.

The test covers eight major categories of content:

Content Categories	Approximate Number of Questions	Approximate Percentage of Examination
Part A (multiple-choice questions):		
I. Child Development and Foundations	14	12%
II. Curriculum and Instruction	17	14%
III. Diversity and Exceptional Needs, and Supporting the Learning Environment	11	9%
IV. Relationships with Families and Communities, and Professionalism	9	7%
V. Assessment	9	7%
Part B (constructed-response questions):		
VI. Diversity and Learning Environment	2	17%
VII. Relationships with Families and Professionalism	2	17%
VIII. Assessment, Curriculum, and Instruction	2	17%

You have two hours to complete the test. It is expected that you will spend roughly equal amounts of time on Parts A and B, but the parts are not timed independently, so you can determine your own pacing based on this recommendation.

The *Pre-Kindergarten Education* (0530) Test

The Praxis *Pre-Kindergarten Education* (0020) test consists of 103 multiple-choice questions. The test assesses both your knowledge of relevant information and your ability to analyze problems and apply principles to specific situations.

The test covers two major categories of content:

Content Categories	Approximate Number of Questions	Approximate Percentage of Examination
I. Development of Young Children and Contributions of Theory to Educational Practices	54	52%
II. Planning, Implementing, and Evaluating Instruction	49	48%

You have two hours to complete the test.

Suggestions for Using This Guide

Q. Why should you use this study guide?

These tests are different from final exams or other tests you may have taken for other courses because they are comprehensive—that is, they cover material you may have learned in several courses during your entire undergraduate program. The tests require you to synthesize information you have learned from many sources and to understand the subject as a whole.

Therefore, you should review and prepare for the test you plan to take, not merely practice with the question formats. A thorough review of the material covered on the test will significantly increase your likelihood of success. Moreover, studying for your licensing exam is a great opportunity to reflect on and develop a deeper understanding of pedagogical and administrative knowledge and methods before you begin your educational career. As you prepare to take the test, it may be particularly helpful for you to think about how you would apply the study topics and sample exercises to your own clinical experience obtained during your teacher preparation program. Your student teaching experience will be especially relevant to your thinking about the materials in the study guide.

Q. How can you best use the "Study Topics" chapter to prepare for the *Education of Young Children* tests?

As you use this book, set the following tasks for yourself:

- **Become familiar with the test content.** Learn what will be tested, as covered in chapter 3.

- **Assess how well you know the content in each area.** After you learn what topics the test contains, you should assess your knowledge in each area. How well do you know the material? In which areas do you need to learn more before you take the test? It is quite likely that you will need to brush up on most or all of the areas. If you encounter material that feels unfamiliar or difficult, fold down page corners or insert sticky notes to remind yourself to spend extra time reviewing these topics.

- **Read chapter 4 to sharpen your skills in reading and answering multiple-choice questions.** To succeed on questions of this kind, you must focus carefully on the question, avoid reading things into the question, pay attention to details, and sift patiently through the answer choices. Chapter 4 shows you the most common formats that are used for multiple-choice questions.

- **Read chapter 5 to learn how to respond to constructed-response questions.** To succeed on questions of this kind, you must understand what specifically is being asked in the question and give a thorough and detailed response. Chapter 5 shows you examples of constructed-response questions and explains what the test scorers look for when they read responses.

- **Develop a study plan.** Assess what you need to study and create a realistic plan for studying. You can develop your study plan in any way that works best for you. A "Study Plan" form is included in appendix A at the end of the book as a possible way to structure your planning. Remember that you will need to allow time to find books and other materials, time to read the materials and take notes, and time to apply your learning to the practice questions.

- **Identify study materials.** Most of the material covered by the test is contained in standard textbooks in the field. If you no longer own the texts you used in your undergraduate course work, you may want to borrow some from friends or from a library. Use standard textbooks and other reliable, professionally prepared materials. Don't rely heavily on information provided by friends or from searching the World Wide Web. Neither of these sources is as uniformly reliable as textbooks. Also review other relevant course materials provided by your instructors.

- **Work through your study plan.** You may want to work alone, or you may find it more helpful to work with a group or with a mentor. Work through the topics and questions provided in chapter 3. Rather than memorizing definitions from books, be able to define and discuss the topics in your own words and understand the relationships between diverse topics and concepts. If you are working with a group or mentor, you can also try informal quizzes and questioning techniques.

- **Proceed to the practice questions.** Once you have completed your review, you are ready to benefit from the practice test in chapter 6 of this guide. Then use the following chapter ("Right Answers and Explanations") to mark the questions you answered correctly and the ones you missed. In this chapter, also look over the explanations of the questions you missed and see whether you understand them.

- **Decide whether you need more review.** After you have looked at your results, decide whether there are areas that you need to brush up on before taking the actual test. Go back to your textbooks and reference materials to see whether the topics are covered there. You might also want to go over your questions with a friend or teacher who is familiar with the subjects.

- **Assess your readiness.** Do you feel confident about your level of understanding in each of the subject areas? If not, where do you need more work? If you feel ready, complete the checklist in chapter 9 to double-check that you've thought through the details. If you need more information about registration or the testing situation itself, use the resources in appendix B: "For More Information."

Q. How might you use this book as part of a study group?

People who have a lot of studying to do sometimes find it helpful to form a study group with others who are preparing toward the same goal. Study groups give members opportunities to ask questions and get detailed answers. In a group, some members usually have a better understanding of certain topics, while others in the group may be better at other topics. As members take turns explaining concepts to each other, everyone builds self-confidence. If the group encounters a question that none of the members can answer well, the members can go as a group to a teacher or other expert and get answers efficiently. Because study groups schedule regular meetings, group members study in a more disciplined fashion. They also gain emotional support. The group should be large enough so that various people can contribute various kinds of knowledge, but small enough so that it stays focused. Often, three to six people make a good-sized group.

Here are some ways to use this book as part of a study group:

- **Plan the group's study program.** Parts of the Study Plan Sheet in appendix A can help to structure your group's study program. By filling out the first five columns and sharing the work sheets, everyone will learn more about your group's mix of abilities and about the resources (such as textbooks) that members can share with the group. In the sixth column ("Dates planned for study of content"), you can create an overall schedule for your group's study program.

- **Plan individual group sessions.** At the end of each session, the group should decide what specific topics will be covered at the next meeting and who will present each topic. Use the topic headings and subheadings in chapter 3.

- **Prepare your presentation for the group.** When it's your turn to be presenter, prepare something that's more than a lecture. Write five to ten original questions to pose to the group. Practicing writing actual questions can help you better understand the topics covered on the test as well as the types of questions you will encounter on the test. It will also give other members of the group extra practice at answering questions.

- **Take the practice test together.** The idea of the practice test in chapter 6 is to simulate an actual administration of the test, so scheduling a test session with the group will add to the realism and will also help boost everyone's confidence.

- **Learn from the results of the practice test.** Use chapter 7 to score each other's answer sheets. Then plan one or more study sessions based on the questions that group members got wrong. For example, each group member might be responsible for a question that he or she got wrong and could use it as a model to create an original question to pose to the group, together with an explanation of the correct answer modeled after the explanations in chapter 7.

Whether you decide to study alone or with a group, remember that the best way to prepare is to have an organized plan. The plan should set goals based on specific topics and skills that you need to learn, and it should commit you to a realistic set of deadlines for meeting these goals. Then you need to discipline yourself to stick with your plan and accomplish your goals on schedule.

Chapter 2

Background Information on The Praxis Series™ Assessments

▶ ▶ ▶ ▶ ▶ ▶ ▶ ▶ ▶ ▶ ▶ ▶

What Are The Praxis Series Assessments?

The Praxis Series Subject Assessments are designed by ETS to assess your knowledge of the area of education in which you plan to work, and they are a part of the licensing procedure in many states. This study guide covers assessments that test your knowledge of the actual content related to your intended specialization. Your state has adopted The Praxis Series tests because it wants to be certain that you have achieved a specified level of mastery of your subject area before it grants you a license to work in a school.

The Praxis Series tests are part of a national testing program, meaning that the tests covered in this study guide are used in more than one state. The advantage of taking Praxis tests is that if you want to practice in another state that uses The Praxis Series tests, that state will recognize your scores. Passing scores are set by states, however, so if you are planning to apply for licensure in another state, you may find that passing scores are different. You can find passing scores for all states that use The Praxis Series tests either online at www.ets.org/praxis/prxstate.html or in the *Understanding Your Praxis Scores* pamphlet, available either in your college's School of Education or by calling 609-771-7395.

What Is Licensure?

Licensure in any area—medicine, law, architecture, accounting, cosmetology—is an assurance to the public that the person holding the license has demonstrated a certain level of competence. The phrase used in licensure is that the person holding the license *will do no harm.* In the case of licensing for educators, a license tells the public that the person holding the license can be trusted to educate children competently and professionally.

Because a license makes such a serious claim about its holder, licensure tests are usually quite demanding. In some fields licensure tests have more than one part and last for more than one day. Candidates for licensure in all fields plan intensive study as part of their professional preparation: some join study groups, while others study alone. But preparing to take a licensure test is, in all cases, a professional activity. Because it assesses your entire body of knowledge or skill for the field you want to enter, preparing for a licensure exam takes planning, discipline, and sustained effort. Studying thoroughly is highly recommended.

Why Does My State Require The Praxis Series Subject Assessments?

Your state chose The Praxis Series Subject Assessments because the tests assess the breadth and depth of content—called the "domain" of the test—that your state wants its education professionals to have before they begin to work. The level of content knowledge, reflected in the passing score, is based on recommendations of panels of professionals and postsecondary educators in each subject area in each state. The state licensing agency and, in some states, the state legislature ratify the passing scores that have been recommended by panels of professionals. (See "What are the Praxis Series Subject Assessments?" above for where to find your state's passing score.) Not all states use the same test modules, and even when they do, the passing scores can differ from state to state.

What Kinds of Tests Are The Praxis Series Subject Assessments?

Two kinds of tests comprise The Praxis Series Subject Assessments: multiple-choice (for which you select your answer from a list of choices) and constructed-response (for which you write a response of your own). Multiple-choice tests can survey a wider domain because they can ask more questions in a limited period of time. Constructed-response tests have far fewer questions, but the questions require you to demonstrate the depth of your knowledge in the area covered.

What Do the Tests Measure?

The Praxis Series Subject Assessments are tests of content knowledge. They measure your understanding of the subject area that will be your specialization. The multiple-choice tests measure a broad range of knowledge across your content area. The constructed-response tests measure your ability to explain in depth a few essential topics in your subject area. The content-specific pedagogy tests, most of which are constructed-response, measure your understanding of how to teach certain fundamental concepts in your field. The tests do not measure actual teaching ability, however. They measure your knowledge of your subject and (for classroom specializations) your knowledge of how to teach it. The professionals in your field who help us design and write these tests, and the states that require these tests, do so in the belief that knowledge of subject area is the first requirement for licensing. Your ability to perform in an actual school is a skill that is measured in other ways: observation, videotaped teaching, or portfolios are typically used by states to measure this ability. Education combines many complex skills, only some of which can be measured by a single test. The Praxis Series Subject Assessments are designed to measure how thoroughly you understand the material in the subject areas for which you want to be licensed.

How Were These Tests Developed?

ETS began the development of The Praxis Series Subject Assessments with a survey. For each subject, professionals around the country in various educational situations were asked to judge which knowledge and skills a beginning practitioner in that subject needs to possess. Professors in schools of education who prepare professionals were asked the same questions. These responses were ranked in order of importance and sent out to hundreds of professionals for review. All of the responses to these surveys (called "job analysis surveys") were analyzed to summarize the judgments of these professionals. From their consensus, we developed the specifications for the multiple-choice and constructed-response tests. Each subject area had a committee of practitioners and postsecondary educators who wrote these specifications (guidelines). The specifications were reviewed and eventually approved by professionals. From the test specifications, groups of practitioners and professional test developers created test questions.

When your state adopted The Praxis Series Subject Assessments, local panels of practicing professionals and postsecondary educators in each subject area met to examine the tests question by question and evaluate each question for its relevance to beginning professionals in your state. This is called a "validity study." A test is considered "valid" for a job if it measures what people must know and be able to do on that job. For the test to be adopted in your state, professionals in your state must judge that it is valid.

These professionals also performed a "standard-setting study"; that is, they went through the tests question by question and decided, through a rigorous process, how many questions a beginning professional should be able to answer correctly. From this study emerged a recommended passing score. The final passing score was approved by your state's Department of Education.

In other words, throughout the development process, practitioners in the field of education—professionals and postsecondary educators—have determined what the tests would contain. The practitioners in your state determined which tests would be used for licensure in your subject area and helped decide what score would be needed to achieve licensure. This is how professional licensure works in most fields: those who are already licensed oversee the licensing of new practitioners. When you pass The Praxis Series Subject Assessments, you and the practitioners in your state can be assured that you have the knowledge required to begin practicing your profession.

Chapter 3
Study Topics for the *Education of Young Children* Tests

You are likely to find that the topics outlined in this chapter are covered by most introductory textbooks in the field of early childhood education, but general survey textbooks may not cover all of the subtopics. Consult materials and resources, including lecture notes, from all your education course work. You should be able to match up specific topics and subtopics with what you have covered in your courses in curriculum design, foundations of education, assessment, and so on.

Try not to be overwhelmed by the volume and scope of content knowledge in this guide. An overview such as this, which presents topics as a list, does not offer you a great deal of context. Although a specific term may not seem familiar as you see it here, you might find that you can understand it when it is applied to a real-life situation. Many of the items on the actual test you take will provide you with a context in which to apply these topics or terms, as you will see when you take the practice test in chapter 6.

Special questions marked with stars

Interspersed throughout the list of topics are questions that are placed in boxes and preceded by stars (★). These questions are intended to help you test your knowledge of fundamental concepts and your ability to apply fundamental concepts to situations in the real world. Most of the questions require you to combine several pieces of knowledge in order to formulate an integrated understanding and response. If you spend time on these questions, you will gain increased understanding and facility with the subject matter covered on the test. You might want to discuss these questions and your answers with a teacher or mentor.

Note that the questions marked with stars are not short-answer or multiple-choice and that this study guide does not provide the answers. The questions marked with stars are intended as *study* questions, not practice questions. Thinking about the answers to them should improve your understanding of fundamental concepts and will probably help you answer a broad range of questions on the test. For example, the following box with a star appears in the list of study topics under the "Social and emotional development" topic:

★ How are the theories of Maslow, Bloom and Piaget similar? How are they different?

If you think about this question, perhaps jotting down some notes on these major theorists and their contributions, you will review your knowledge of the subject and you will probably be ready to answer multiple-choice questions similar to the one below:

According to Abraham Maslow, a child who frequently comes to school hungry, tired, and dressed in dirty clothing has which of the following unmet needs?

(A) Self-actualization
(B) Self-esteem
(C) Safety and security
(D) Physiological
(E) Love and belongingness

The correct answer is (D). Hunger and lack of sleep signify unmet physiological needs. This child may also have unmet needs in the categories named in the other choices, but no information is provided about the choices, so they can be only logical (but unsubstantiated) inferences at best.

Here is an overview of the topics covered on the test, along with their subtopics. On each test, you will typically find a number of questions on each of the subtopics described in the bulleted items. Note that the outlined subtopics introduce ideas but do not necessarily include all possible related ideas. For example, under "Stages of physical development," you will find bullets for "Gross and fine motor development" and "Brain development." The fact that "Development of height and weight" and other kinds of physical development are not also included does not mean that they are irrelevant to this topic.

Child Development and Foundations

An understanding of child development and foundations is crucial for those involved in the education of young children. Child development involves not only physical, cognitive, social, emotional, and language development, but also influences on development and how those influences affect learning. Decisions concerning the education of young children must be made within the context of the child's development in order to maximize learning and avoid inappropriate instruction.

Childhood physical development

- Stages of physical development
  - Gross and fine motor development
  - Brain development

- Implications for learning

- Major progressions in each developmental domain
  - Ranges of individual variation within each domain

- Atypical physical development of young children

★ What are the stages of gross and fine motor development?

★ How would you adapt a learning activity to the physical development of a 3-year-old child versus the development of an 8-year-old child?

★ What would be within the range of individual variation for a 5-year-old child's fine motor development?

★ What would be considered atypical fine motor development for a 5-year-old child?

Cognitive development

- Important theorists
  - Bruner
  - Bandura
  - Bloom
  - Piaget

- Methods students use to solve problems at various stages of cognitive development

- Influences on cognitive abilities
  - Environmental
  - Hereditary

- Chronological-age-appropriate behavior

★ Compare and contrast the theories of Bruner, Bandura, Bloom, and Piaget.

★ How would the method by which a 4-year-old child solves a problem differ from that of a 7-year-old child?

★ What are some ways in which environment and inheritance shape cognitive ability?

Social and emotional development

- Important theorists
  - Maslow
  - Bloom
  - Piaget
  - Vygotsky

- Erikson's stages of emotional growth

- Factors that influence social and emotional development
  - Gender
  - Home life
  - Cultural identity
  - Role models

★ How are the theories of Maslow, Bloom, and Piaget similar? How are they different?

★ List Erikson's stages of emotional growth and indicate a behavior that would be representative of each stage. Indicate a behavior that would be atypical for each stage.

★ Indicate several ways in which gender, home life, cultural identify, and role models influence social and emotional development.

Language development

- Factors that shape oral language development

- Factors that foster literacy skills

★ Describe an early childhood learning environment that would shape oral language development.

★ What should be included in preschool and primary grades to foster literacy skills?

Influences on development and learning

- Factors that influence physical, cognitive, and emotional development in the child's home and community life

  ▶ Nutrition
  ▶ Health
  ▶ Disabilities
  ▶ Socioeconomic status
  ▶ Cultural upbringing
  ▶ Family and community values

- Developmentally appropriate learning opportunities that influence a child's growth and development

- Milestones of social and cognitive growth

  ▶ How to observe these in a child who is playing alone and/or with peers

- Major theories concerning development

  ▶ Constructivist
  ▶ Maturationist
  ▶ Sociocultural
  ▶ Behaviorist
  ▶ Ecological
  ▶ Contributions of cognitive learning theorists

★ List five ways in which nutrition, health, disabilities, socioeconomic status, cultural upbringing, and family and community values can influence a child's physical, cognitive, and emotional development.

★ Why is play important for development and learning?

★ What important points should be presented to counteract the argument that play does not belong in a school environment?

★ Take one concept—e.g., one-to-one correspondence in mathematics—and describe how the major cognitive learning theorists would present a learning opportunity for a primary-grade child. Include the major cognitive learning theories concerning development (i.e., constructivist, maturationist, sociocultural, behaviorist, and ecological).

Curriculum and Instruction

Curriculum and instruction cover a wide range of areas, from general instruction to specific subjects. It is important that the educator of young children understand not only what to teach, but also when and how to teach. Knowledge is no longer compartmentalized into just mathematics or just literacy; rather, education attempts to interconnect concepts across the curriculum. For example, science is the understanding of scientific concepts as explained by mathematical methods and linguistic interpretation. Learning is related to both knowledge of the subject matter and an understanding of the process. The educator must have a strong knowledge both of specific material and of the process that encompasses human cognition and learning in order to integrate knowledge acquisition into one cohesive whole for the young child.

General instruction

- The curriculum process
  - ▶ Structuring a curriculum
  - ▶ Implementing a curriculum
  - ▶ Revising or modifying a curriculum
  - ▶ Aligning a curriculum to reflect state standards
- How routines and transitions reflect a young child's needs
  - ▶ Balance
  - ▶ Order
  - ▶ Depth
  - ▶ Variety
  - ▶ Structure
  - ▶ Challenge
  - ▶ Physical activity
- Instructional strategies
  - ▶ Play
  - ▶ Small groups
  - ▶ Cooperative learning
  - ▶ Inquiry
  - ▶ Discovery learning
  - ▶ Learning centers
  - ▶ Teacher-directed learning
  - ▶ Theme
  - ▶ Directed reading
- Major theories and models of programmed instruction
  - ▶ Constructivism
  - ▶ Montessori
  - ▶ Project Approach

- ▶ High/Scope
- ▶ Reggio Emilia

- Curriculum integration as it relates to instruction

- Cognitive tasks demanded from a lesson, teaching practice, or questioning technique

- How to elicit and encourage in-depth responses and metacognitive thinking from children at age-appropriate levels

- Techniques for creating effective bridges between curriculum goals and students' previous experiences (or lack of previous experiences)

★ Design a series of literacy lessons for early childhood education and indicate the state standards for which the lessons have been aligned.

★ Develop activities that involve a variety of instructional strategies and focus on one learning concept (e.g., how play, inquiry, and learning centers could be used to teach number concepts to 4-year-old children).

★ Design a learning activity that incorporates science, mathematics, and literacy. Indicate which areas of the curriculum will be integrated into the lesson.

★ What would be some appropriate questions that would elicit in-depth responses and encourage children to focus on their thinking strategies? What would be inappropriate questions for young children?

★ What previous experiences should students have been exposed to prior to a lesson on addition?

Mathematics/numeracy

- Developmentally appropriate practices in lessons based on mathematical concepts
  - ▶ Design
  - ▶ Implementation
  - ▶ Evaluation

- Mathematical concepts
  - ▶ Estimation
  - ▶ Geometry
  - ▶ Number sense and numeration
  - ▶ Whole-number operations

★ Design a lesson for 5-year-old children that will introduce basic geometrical concepts. What instructional strategies would you use? How would you evaluate the effectiveness of your lesson?

★ Identify a state standard for each of the following mathematical concepts: estimation, geometry, number sense and numeration, and whole-number operations.

Literacy

- Developmentally appropriate practice in lessons that promote oral language expression and literacy in children
  - ▶ Design
  - ▶ Implementation
  - ▶ Evaluation

- Importance of providing children with a literacy-rich environment
  - ▶ Printed material
    - – As sources of information
    - – For pleasure or recreation
    - – As a means of recording or communicating
  - ▶ Availability of reading, writing, and listening materials, computers, printers, and audiovisual equipment

- Specific literacy concepts
  - ▶ Writing process
  - ▶ Phonemic awareness
  - ▶ Sentence decoding
  - ▶ Word families
  - ▶ Root words
  - ▶ Phonics

- Characteristics of quality children's books
  - ▶ Balanced collections that reflect a wide variety of genres and reflect the makeup of the community
  - ▶ Books that have strong story lines, age-appropriate themes, illustrations, and/or read-aloud possibilities

- Specific literacy teaching strategies
  - ▶ Grapheme-phoneme correspondence
  - ▶ Journal writing
  - ▶ Shared reading
  - ▶ Cueing systems
  - ▶ Rubrics
  - ▶ Reflective logs

★ Describe a literacy-rich environment for young children. Explain how the components of the environment will foster literacy concepts.

★ Design a unit that incorporates the writing process into daily activities. Specify each stage of the writing process within the unit.

★ How do phonemic awareness, sentence decoding, word families, root words, and phonics support literacy development? Identify each of these specific literacy concepts and the role each plays in literacy development.

★ Identify each of the following literacy teaching strategies and how each strategy could be used to help a student for whom English is a second language: grapheme-phoneme correspondence, journal writing, shared reading, cueing systems, rubrics, and reflective logs.

Science

- Developmentally appropriate practice in lessons that develop each child's innate curiosity about the world and broaden each child's procedural and thinking skills for investigating the world, solving problems, and making decisions
    - Design
    - Implementation
    - Evaluation
- General principles of scientific inquiry
    - Cause and effect
    - Systems
    - Scale
    - Models
    - Change
    - Variations
    - Structure and function

★ Choose a grade level and design an Earth science unit that identifies goals, state standards, activities, and evaluation.

★ Think about ways in which the principles of scientific inquiry can be employed for developing a child's innate curiosity about the world, for broadening a child's procedural and thinking skills for investigating the world, solving problems, and making decisions.

Social studies/character inquiry

- Developmentally appropriate practice in learning experiences that promote cultural and character education
    - Design
    - Implementation
    - Evaluation
- Ability to design, implement, and evaluate lessons that develop the social studies disciplines
    - History

- Geography
- Economics

★ Design an activity that promotes cultural and character education. Include extension activities and evaluation procedures.

★ Develop an activity that would involve multiple social studies disciplines (e.g., history, geography, and economics).

Creative arts/aesthetics

- Developmentally appropriate practice in visual and performing arts lessons that engage and broaden each child's experiences and skills
    - Design
    - Implementation
    - Evaluation
- Ability to integrate the arts into content area studies
- Appropriate responses to children's work

★ Design a learning activity for visual and performing arts that would be appropriate for a 5-year-old child. Identify the learning goal for this activity and the means for evaluating the success of this goal.

★ Develop a unit that integrates the arts into content area studies. Include activities that integrate the arts with mathematics, literacy, science, and social studies.

★ How can creative arts and aesthetics be used to enhance learning in other content areas?

★ What is the value of creative arts and aesthetics in education?

★ Should creative arts and aesthetics be integrated with content area studies? Identify several ways in which creative arts and aesthetics enhance learning. Are there times when creative arts and aesthetics might hinder learning?

Physical education/health

- Developmentally appropriate practice in the content discipline designed to strengthen gross and fine motor skills and foster healthy lifestyles

- Safety procedures and precautions

- Impact of medical conditions and procedures to handle such conditions
  - ▶ Epilepsy
  - ▶ Diabetes
  - ▶ Use of injectable medications to prevent allergic reactions
  - ▶ Handling of blood

★ What are some activities that could be conducted in physical education sessions to strengthen a 5-year-old student's fine motor skills?

★ What is the relationship between gross and fine motor skill development?

★ Design a unit on gross motor skills for 6-year-old students. What safety procedures and precautions should be considered in developing this unit?

★ Outline the important points that would need to be discussed during an in-service workshop on the impact of medical conditions and the procedures for handling such conditions. Include information concerning epilepsy, diabetes, use of an EpiPen® for severe allergies, and handling of blood.

★ What safety information should be conveyed to teachers?

★ What safety information should be shared with students to ensure their safety and understanding of medical conditions?

Technology

- Appropriate use of technology in the early childhood classroom

- How to adapt technology for use with students with special needs

- Ability to evaluate effective use of technology in the early childhood classroom

★ Describe an early childhood classroom that provides students with a variety of opportunities to interact with technology. Include one activity for each form of technology, specifically indicating the form of technology and how technology will enhance learning for the students.

★ How can technology be adapted for use with students with special needs? Indicate adaptations for physical, emotional, and educational needs.

★ Develop a unit that will incorporate technology with literacy. Indicate specific activities that will enhance literacy learning. Develop assessment tools that will evaluate the effective use of technology to attain the specified goals.

Diversity and Exceptional Needs, and Supporting the Learning Environment

Education must encompass the diverse needs of all students. It is the responsibility of the teacher to establish a learning environment that not only allows but also encourages every child to reach optimal learning. Accommodations must be made to meet the needs of each child and to create a developmentally appropriate setting for learning. The teacher must understand the individual needs of every student and create an environment in which every child has an opportunity for success.

Students as diverse learners

- Exceptionality in students' learning
  - ▶ Visual and perceptual difficulties
  - ▶ Learning disabilities
  - ▶ Attention deficit disorder (ADD)
  - ▶ Attention-deficit/hyperactivity disorder (ADHD)

- Accommodations for students with special educational needs and for children whose first language is not English

- Approaches for accommodating various learning styles and intelligences

- Issues of cultural sensitivity and responsiveness to gender and equity issues

- Effective integration of multicultural activities into the classroom curriculum

- Curricular contexts affecting choice of instructional strategies
  - ▶ Child population
  - ▶ Adaptations
  - ▶ Special needs
  - ▶ Local community
  - ▶ Local cultures
  - ▶ Physical environment

- How instruction should be connected with children's personal experiences

---

★ What are the basic characteristics of children with special needs in an early childhood setting with respect to visual and perceptual difficulties, learning disabilities, attention deficit disorder (ADD), and attention-deficit/hyperactivity disorder (ADHD)?

★ Choose an age level and develop a literacy lesson that would introduce story structure. Include activities that would be appropriate for a small group of children that includes a student with perceptual difficulties and another student whose first language is not English.

★ How could technology be used to accommodate various learning styles and intelligences during a unit on science?

★ How could cultural sensitivity and gender and equity issues be incorporated into a preschool program? Design a unit that specifically deals with these issues, and include a connection to the children's personal experiences.

Creating a developmentally appropriate setting

- Recognizing health and safety issues
  - ▶ Basic sanitation
  - ▶ Nutrition
  - ▶ Room ventilation
  - ▶ Good health practices

- How to arrange the indoor and outdoor spatial environments effectively
  - ▶ Individual activities
  - ▶ Cooperative activities
  - ▶ Small- and whole-group activities
  - ▶ Providing opportunities for children to play, explore, and discover

- Understanding and accommodating various children's needs based on different learning styles

  ▶ Visual

  ▶ Auditory

  ▶ Tactile

  ▶ Kinesthetic

- Structuring the environment to accommodate students with physical and emotional disabilities

  ▶ Placement of vision- and hearing-impaired students

  ▶ Space and paths for wheelchairs

  ▶ Children with challenging behaviors

  ▶ Functional behavior assessment guidelines

- Recognizing the child's role in creating the environment and assuming ownership

---

★ How do health and safety issues affect learning? Include the effects of basic sanitation, nutrition, room ventilation, and good health practices.

★ Design learning environments, both indoor and outdoor, that allow for individual, cooperative, small- and whole-group activities, as well as providing opportunities for children to play, explore, and discover. Indicate one learning activity for each spatial environment.

★ Design one learning activity. Indicate how that learning activity could include visual, auditory, tactile, and kinesthetic modes. Be able to explain why it is important to consider the varied learning styles of the students.

★ Design a classroom that would accommodate students with physical and emotional disabilities, including, but not limited to, placement of vision- and hearing-impaired students, space and paths for wheelchairs, children with challenging behaviors, and functional behavior assessment guidelines.

★ What support could be given to a child with challenging behaviors to help that child both as an individual and as a person within a class? Indicate the child's role as well as the roles of the child's classmates in creating the environment and assuming ownership.

Creating a socially stimulating environment

- Designing an environment that provides children with a sense of well-being, belonging, ownership, and freedom from physical and psychological fear

- Importance of developing a positive prosocial classroom tone

  ▶ Possessing a repertoire of guidance approaches to meet individual children's needs

  ▶ Effects of language and tone on children

  ▶ Acting as a role model who facilitates learning

★ List five steps a teacher could take to design an environment that provides children with a sense of well-being, belonging, ownership, and freedom from physical and psychological fear.

★ What would be the appropriate way for a teacher to react to a 6-year-old child who constantly interrupts class discussions?

★ How do role models facilitate learning? Who can act as a role model other than the teacher in a learning environment? Be specific in identifying means of facilitation and the role models.

Relationships with Families and Communities, and Professionalism

Effective learning encompasses not just the classroom, but also the family and community. To be successful, the educational process must be supported in the home and the community. Reinforcing the value of education conveys to the child the importance of learning and encourages the child to strive for additional knowledge. It is the responsibility of the teacher to convey information concerning the learning process to the family and the community and to coordinate the goals for both school and home. A high level of professionalism, as well as teacher self-assessment, is crucial in maintaining this relationship with families and communities.

Respectful, reciprocal relationships with families and communities

- Family and community characteristics
  - Family structure
  - Socioeconomic conditions
  - Home language
  - Ethnicity
  - Religion
  - Culture
  - Stresses and supports, such as special needs, births, deaths, or divorce

- Basic strategies for involving parents or guardians in the educational process
  - Valuing family input
  - Recognizing the family as the child's first teacher
  - Identifying multiple ways to support families' efforts to help children learn
  - Creating a welcoming environment that promotes family involvement and partnerships

- The importance of proactive communication and collaboration
  - Ongoing discussions and conferences
  - Procedures to protect the confidentiality of a family
  - Sharing of curriculum, policy, and procedures
  - Identifying available agencies and community resources
  - Connecting resources with families who need them
  - Collaborating with in-school professionals

- The role of school as a resource to the larger community
  - Community resources such as businesses and public agencies
  - Strategies for accessing community resources .
  - How partnerships and mentoring can enhance learning
  - How children can contribute to the community

★ How is a child's learning affected by family and community characteristics, such as family structure, socioeconomic conditions, home language, ethnicity, religion, or culture, and stresses and supports, such as special needs, births, deaths, or divorce? Indicate five ways in which a teacher could be informed of these characteristics without violating the privacy of individual families.

★ Indicate one activity for using each of these basic strategies that involves parents or guardians in the educational process: valuing family input, recognizing the family as the child's first teacher, identifying multiple ways to support families' efforts to help children learn, and creating a welcoming environment that promotes family involvement and partnerships.

★ Design an activity that would create a welcoming environment that promotes family involvement and partnerships.

★ Indicate one activity for each of the following means of proactive communication and collaboration: ongoing discussions and conferences; procedures to protect the confidentiality of a family; sharing of curriculum, policy, and procedures; identifying the available agencies and community resources and connecting them with families who need them; and collaborating with in-school professionals.

★ Design an outline for a parent conference concerning one of your students. Indicate five strengths that you have observed in the student. List three areas that parents could reinforce at home. Be specific concerning the parental support, indicating materials and methods that the parents could utilize.

★ How could a preschool program use community resources to enhance student learning? Indicate five ways to access community resources and five ways in which students could contribute to the community.

Professionalism

- The importance of ethical behavior in both personal and professional practice

  ► Major laws related to students' rights and teacher responsibilities

  ► IDEA '97

  ► Confidentiality and privacy

  ► Appropriate education of students with disabilities

  ► Child abuse reporting

  ► Assessment

- The importance of continuing professional development, including professional memberships

- Collaboration with colleagues and paraprofessionals

- Effective advocacy for children

★ What is the importance of IDEA '97?

★ List five reasons why it is important to continue professional development, including professional memberships.

★ How would conferring with colleagues and paraprofessionals help in understanding a student's needs?

★ What are the responsibilities of a teacher in serving as an effective advocate for children?

Self-assessment

- The importance of using self-assessment techniques to reflect on teaching practices and the learning environment

★ Indicate three ways in which a teacher can use self-assessment techniques to reflect on teaching practices and the learning environment.

★ How can self-assessment improve a successful lesson?

★ How can self-assessment improve a lesson that failed to meet the designated goals?

Assessment

Learning and teaching are parts of an ongoing process in which goals are established, activities are designed, and outcomes are assessed to determine success. At each stage, the next goals are established according to assessment results in a constant cycle of learning and assessing. It is important that a teacher understand the variety of assessment tools and their purposes in order to align assessment with teaching goals, activities, and curriculum. It is also important that the teacher be effective in conveying information concerning assessment to families and other professionals.

- Different types of assessments and their purposes

  - ► Formal and informal
  - ► Standardized
  - ► Criterion referenced
  - ► Summative
  - ► Formative
  - ► Developmental screening
  - ► Portfolios/work samples
  - ► Rubrics
  - ► Observation
  - ► Anecdotal records
  - ► Running records
  - ► Interviews

- Multiple sources of information as useful in determining individual strengths and needs

  - ► Use of ongoing and systematic assessment strategies, both summative and formative
  - ► Use of authentic assessment

- How to align assessment with teaching goals and curriculum

- The ability to make fair and reasonable judgments about student learning and about situations in which inappropriate assessment may harm children

- Ways in which children can be involved in the assessment process

- The importance of sharing assessment results with families and communicating the meaning of different types of assessment results

★ Identify the important characteristics and purposes for each of the following different types of assessments: formal and informal, standardized, criterion referenced, summative, and formative tests; developmental screening; portfolios/work samples; rubrics; observation; anecdotal records, running records; interviews. Indicate the role of each assessment in the education of preschool or primary-grade students.

★ What is the difference between summative and formative assessment? Identify a tool for each assessment. When would a summative assessment be appropriate? When would a formative assessment provide more information?

★ Identify a learning goal and an authentic assessment that would determine the effectiveness of an activity in meeting this goal. Be specific in identifying the authentic assessment and how information from the assessment would be used in developing future learning goals.

★ What are ways in which bias would affect the assessment of student learning? Include both positive and negative bias and the effect of each on the learning process.

★ How can young children be involved in the assessment process?

★ Indicate four ways in which assessment results can be communicated to families effectively. Provide guidelines that would help parents understand how to use this information to support their children's learning.

Chapter 4
Don't Be Defeated by Multiple-Choice Questions

► ► ► ► ► ► ► ► ► ► ► ►

Understanding Multiple-Choice Questions

When you read multiple-choice questions on the Praxis *Early Childhood Education* test or on Part A of the *Education of Young Children* test, you will probably notice that the syntax (word order) is different from the word order you're used to seeing in ordinary material that you read, such as newspapers or textbooks. One of the reasons for this difference is that many test questions contain the phrase "which of the following."

In order to answer a multiple-choice question successfully, you need to consider carefully the context set up by the question and limit your choice of answers to the list given. The purpose of the phrase "which of the following" is to remind you to do this. For example, look at this question.

> Which of the following is a flavor made from beans?
>
> (A) Strawberry
> (B) Cherry
> (C) Vanilla
> (D) Mint

You may know that chocolate and coffee are also flavors made from beans, but they are not listed, and the question asks you to select from the list that follows ("which of the following"). So the answer has to be the only bean-derived flavor in the list: vanilla.

Notice that the answer can be substituted for the phrase "which of the following." In the question above, you could insert "vanilla" for "which of the following" and have the sentence "Vanilla is a flavor made from beans." Sometimes it helps to cross out "which of the following" and insert the various choices. You may want to give this technique a try as you answer various multiple-choice questions on the practice test.

Looking carefully at the "which of the following" phrase helps you to focus on what the question is asking you to find and on the answer choices. In the simple example above, all of the answer choices are flavors. Your job is to decide which of the flavors is the one made from beans.

The vanilla bean question is pretty straightforward. But the phrase "which of the following" can also be found in more challenging questions. Look at this question:

> Which of the following teacher actions would best support the development of literacy skills in the early elementary classroom?
>
> (A) Using a commercially developed language arts curriculum aligned with national standards
> (B) Creating attractive bulletin boards using commercially prepared materials
> (C) Teaching phonics, decoding, and word-recognition skills using work sheets
> (D) Providing children with motivating reading and writing materials and assignments

The placement of "which of the following" tells you that the list of choices is a list of examples (in this case, these are examples of things a teacher might do in an early elementary classroom). What are you supposed to find as an answer? You are supposed to find the choice that best supports the development of literacy skills.

ETS question writers and editors work very hard to word each question as clearly as possible. Sometimes, though, it helps to put the question in your own words. Here, you could paraphrase the question as "Which of these techniques would help my students most with their literacy skills?" The correct answer is D. (Research has found that providing students with varied opportunities to engage in the reading and writing processes stimulates their motivation and advances their reading skills. Teaching phonics skills in isolation using work sheets may teach letter-sound relationships, but not the literacy skills of reading and writing. There is little indication that commercial curriculums and commercially produced classroom materials help students learn to read.)

You may also find that it helps you to circle or underline each of the critical details of the question in your test book so that you don't miss any of them. It's only by looking at all parts of the question carefully that you will have all of the information you need to answer it. Circle or underline the critical parts of what is being asked in this question.

Which of the following strategies will best foster multiculturalism in the classroom?

(A) Playing a variety of music from different cultures
(B) Providing foods from various countries in the role-play area
(C) Inviting families to share their customs with the class
(D) Hanging travel posters from various countries in the classroom

Here is one possible way you may have annotated the question:

Which of the following <u>strategies</u> will best | foster multiculturalism | in the classroom?

(A) Playing a variety of music from different cultures
(B) Providing foods from various countries in the role-play area
(C) Inviting families to share their customs with the class
(D) Hanging travel posters from various countries in the classroom

After thinking about the question, you can probably see that you are being asked to look at a list of classroom techniques and decide which one gives students the greatest awareness of other cultures. The correct answer is C. The important thing is understanding what the question is asking. With enough practice, you should be able to determine what any question is asking. Knowing the answer is, of course, a different matter, but you have to understand a question before you can answer it correctly.

Understanding questions containing "NOT," "LEAST," or "EXCEPT"

The words "NOT," "LEAST," and "EXCEPT" can make comprehension of test questions more difficult. A question containing one of these words asks you to select the choice that *doesn't* fit. You must be very careful with this question type because it's easy to forget that you're selecting the negative. This question type is used in situations in which there are several good solutions, or ways to approach something, but also a clearly wrong way. These words are always capitalized when they appear in The Praxis Series test questions, but they are easily (and frequently) overlooked.

For the following test question, determine what kind of answer you need and what the details of the question are.

> All of the following are accurate generalizations about children's biological development EXCEPT:
>
> (A) Sex differences in growth are relatively small during the infant and early childhood years.
>
> (B) Children's hand preference develops around 2 years of age.
>
> (C) Children's physical characteristics tend to be more like those of the mother than those of the father.
>
> (D) While most children follow the same sequence of growth, they may differ considerably in their rates of maturation.
>
> (E) The average height and weight of children in the United States have both increased over the last century.

You're looking for a general statement about children's biological development that is NOT accurate. C is the correct answer—all of the other choices *are* true about children's biological development.

TIP
It's easy to get confused while you're processing the information to answer a question with a LEAST, NOT, or EXCEPT in the question. If you treat the word "LEAST," "NOT," or "EXCEPT" as one of the details you must satisfy, you have a better chance of understanding what the question is asking.

Be Familiar with Multiple-Choice Question Types

You will probably see more than one question format on a multiple-choice test. Here are examples of some of the more common question formats.

Complete the statement

In this type of question, you are given an incomplete statement. You must select the choice that will make the completed statement correct.

> After using the words "tooth" and "teeth" correctly, some children begin saying "tooths" and "teeths." This usage results from
>
> (A) paralanguage
>
> (B) difficulty in producing language
>
> (C) overgeneralization
>
> (D) poor listening skills

To check your answer, reread the question and add your answer choice at the end. Be sure that your choice best completes the sentence. The correct answer is (C).

Which of the following

This question type is discussed in detail in a previous section. The question contains the details that must be satisfied for a correct answer, and it uses "which of the following" to limit the choices to the four choices shown, as this example demonstrates.

> Jimmy, who is in preschool, is able to take off and put on his coat independently during the school day. However, when his mother picks him up, he expects her to help him get dressed. Which of the following would be the most appropriate teacher comment in this situation?
>
> (A) "May I ask why are you putting Jimmy's coat on for him?"
> (B) "If you put on Jimmy's coat, he will not do it for himself."
> (C) "Jimmy can now put on his coat by himself."
> (D) "It's important that you let Jimmy take care of himself."

The correct answer is (C).

Roman numeral choices

This format is used when there can be more than one correct answer in the list. Consider the following example.

> Which of the following items are appropriate to include in students' personal portfolios, which a teacher uses to assess the students?
>
> I. Dated work samples with teacher commentaries
> II. Anecdotal records and records of systematic observations
> III. Checklists, rating scales, and screening inventories
> IV. Weekly classroom lesson plans and curriculum goals
>
> (A) I and II only
> (B) II and III only
> (C) I, II, and III only
> (D) I, III, and IV only

One useful strategy for this type of question is to assess each possible answer before looking at the answer choices and then evaluate the answer choices. In the question above, "Dated work samples accompanied by teacher commentary" are appropriate for inclusion in an assessment portfolio. So are "Anecdotal records and records of systematic observations" and "Checklists, rating scales, and screening inventories." "Weekly classroom lesson plans and curriculum goals," however, do not belong in an assessment portfolio. Therefore, the correct answer is (C).

Questions containing "NOT," "LEAST," or "EXCEPT"

This question type is discussed at length above. It asks you to select the choice that doesn't fit. You must be very careful with this question type because it's easy to forget that you're selecting the negative. This question type is used in situations in which there are several good solutions, or ways to approach something, but also a clearly wrong way.

Other formats

New formats are developed from time to time in order to find new ways of assessing knowledge with multiple-choice questions. If you see a format you are not familiar with, read the directions carefully. Then read and approach the question the way you would any other question, asking yourself what you are supposed to be looking for and what details are given in the question that help you find the answer.

Other Useful Facts about the Test

1. **You can answer the questions in any order.** You can go through the questions from beginning to end, as many test takers do, or you can create your own path. Perhaps you will want to answer questions in your strongest area of knowledge first and then move from your strengths to your weaker areas. There is no right or wrong way. Use the approach that works best for you.

2. **There are no trick questions on the test.** You don't have to find any hidden meanings or worry about trick wording. All of the questions on the test ask about subject matter knowledge in a straightforward manner.

3. **Don't worry about answer patterns.** There is one myth that says that answers on multiple-choice tests follow patterns. There is another myth that there will never be more than two questions with the same lettered answer following each other. There is no truth to either of these myths. Select the answer you think is correct based on your knowledge of the subject.

4. **There is no penalty for guessing.** Your test score for multiple-choice questions is based on the number of correct answers you have. When you don't know the answer to a question, try to eliminate any obviously wrong answers and then guess at the correct one.

5. **It's OK to write in your test booklet.** You can work out problems right on the pages of the booklet, make notes to yourself, mark questions you want to review later, or write anything at all. Your test booklet will be destroyed after you are finished with it, so use it in any way that is helpful to you. But make sure to mark your answers on the answer sheet.

Smart Tips for Taking the Test

1. **Put your answers in the right "bubbles."** It seems obvious, but be sure that you are filling in the answer "bubble" that corresponds to the question you are answering. A significant number of test takers fill in a bubble without checking to see that the number matches the question they are answering.

2. **Skip the questions you find extremely difficult.** There are sure to be some questions that you think are hard. Rather than trying to answer these on your first pass through the test, leave them blank and mark them in your test booklet so that you can come back to them later. Pay attention to the time as you answer the rest of the questions on the test, and try to finish with 10 or 15 minutes remaining so that you can go back over the questions you left blank. Even if you don't know the answer the second time you read the questions, see if you can narrow down the possible answers, and then guess.

3. **Keep track of the time.** Bring a watch to the test, just in case the clock in the test room is difficult for you to see. You will probably have plenty of time to answer all of the questions, but if you find yourself becoming bogged down in one section, you might decide to move on and come back to that section later.

4. **Read all of the possible answers before selecting one**—and then reread the question to be sure the answer you have selected really answers the question being asked. Remember that a question that contains a phrase such as "Which of the following does NOT..." is asking for the one answer that is NOT a correct statement or conclusion.

5. **Check your answers.** If you have extra time left over at the end of the test, look over each question and make sure that you have filled in the "bubble" on the answer sheet as you intended. Many test takers make careless mistakes that they could have corrected if they had checked their answers.

6. **Don't worry about your score when you are taking the test.** No one is expected to answer all of the questions correctly. Your score on this test is *not* analogous to your score on the SAT, the GRE, or other similar-looking (but in fact very different!) tests. It doesn't matter on this test whether you score very high or barely pass. If you meet the minimum passing scores for your state and you meet the state's other requirements for obtaining a teaching license, you will receive a license. In other words, your actual score doesn't matter, as long as it is above the minimum required score. With your score report you will receive a booklet entitled *Understanding Your Praxis Scores,* which lists the passing scores for your state.

7. **Use your energy to take the test, not to get angry at it.** Getting angry at the test only elevates test anxiety, decreasing the likelihood that you will do your best on the test. Highly qualified educators and test development professionals (all with backgrounds in teaching) worked diligently to make the test the best it could be. Your state had the test painstakingly reviewed before adopting it as a licensure requirement. The best thing to do is concentrate on answering the questions as well as you can. Take the test, do your best, pass it, and get on with your career.

Chapter 5
Succeeding on the Constructed-Response Portion of the *Education of Young Children* Test

▶ ▶ ▶ ▶ ▶ ▶ ▶ ▶ ▶ ▶ ▶ ▶

The goal of this chapter is to help you improve your skills in writing answers to constructed-response questions related to the education of young children. You will see advice from experts, a close examination of a sample question, and background information on how the tests are scored.

Advice from the Experts

Scorers who have scored hundreds of real tests were asked to give advice to students taking the *Education of Young Children* test. The scorers' advice boils down to the practical pieces of advice given below.

1. **Read carefully through the question before you answer it, and try to answer all parts of the question.**

    This seems simple, but many test takers fail to understand the question and provide a complete response. If the question asks for three activities, don't forget to discuss three. If the question asks for problems and solutions, don't describe just problems. No matter how well you write about *one* part of the question, the scorers cannot award you full credit unless you answer the question completely and correctly.

2. **Show that you understand both the subject-matter concepts related to the question and how to teach them.**

    The scorers are looking to see not only that you understand the concepts related to the questions, but also that you can apply this knowledge through appropriate strategies to situations in early childhood education. You can show your understanding these concepts not merely by mentioning that the concepts exist, but also by explaining them as you would to students and relating them to the specifics of your response.

    For example, in answering a question about planning an integrated unit on weather for the diverse learners in your kindergarten class, you should not merely restate that the diverse learners in your kindergarten class are learning about weather through an integrated unit; this only repeats the question's text and would not give activities that are reflective of an integrated unit. You should explain that an understanding of weather in young children is dependent upon their observations over time and their participation in seasonal activities in all areas of instruction. You could also improve on this answer by providing specific examples of activities, such as saying that the children will use a bar graph to show the number of snowy days in a month, which is appropriate for the age level you are addressing.

3. **Show that you have a thorough understanding of the specific terms in the question.**

    Some answers receive partial credit because they are vague—they address the topic at too general a level rather than at a level that takes into consideration the particulars implied by the educational terms being used.

    Example #1: *The question asks you to list FOUR materials that the parents would see in a learning center that will promote visual and auditory skills related to reading.* Do not make vague references about reading in general, such as the fact that the students are at the emerging stage in their reading skills, but instead focus on the basic principles of visual and auditory skills needed for reading—for example, by discussing environmental print and identifying store logos or listening to a tape-recorded story and answering questions about the story.

Example #2: *The question asks you about teaching the concept of counting in mathematics.* Don't answer the question in terms of mathematics in general, such as stating that young children should rote count numbers from 1 to 10. Instead, focus on a specific definition of counting and communicate an understanding of this definition through strategies and techniques used in counting that would contribute to student learning. Discuss counting the number of steps as the children climb to the top of the slide and commenting on "how many steps" they climbed, or counting the crackers they will eat for snack and who will eat "more crackers."

A thorough answer also provides the scorer with evidence that you know the specific terms and instructional practices related to the questions. Do not simply use the terms in a generic sentence that could work for any number of terms. Convince the scorers that you understand the terms and can apply them appropriately in instructional situations.

4. **Support your answers with appropriate details.**

The scorers are looking for justification of your answers. Support your answer with details that demonstrate your level of understanding and with materials and activities asked for in the question that are appropriate for the age level (e.g., reflecting on the part-whole relationship underlying addition, such as the idea that a whole cookie is greater than any single piece, advances mathematical thinking in young children, while memorization of number facts by rote does not).

By providing appropriate details, examples, and additional information, you help to clarify answers that may be unusual or may be interpreted in other ways.

A word of caution: Superfluous writing will obscure your points and will make it difficult for the scorers to be confident of your full understanding of the material. Be straightforward in your response. Do not try to impress the scorers. If you do not know the answer, you cannot receive full credit; but if you do know the answer, provide enough information to convince the scorers that you have a full understanding of the topic.

5. **Do not change the question or challenge the basis of the question.**

Stay focused on the question that is asked, and do your best to answer it. You will receive no credit or, at best, a low score if you choose to answer another question or if you state, for example, that there is no possible answer.

Answer the question by addressing the fundamental issues. Do not venture off-topic to demonstrate your particular field of expertise if it is not specifically related to the question. This undermines the impression that you understand the concept adequately.

6. **Wherever applicable, demonstrate that you understand, in addition to the basic developmental concepts and terms, the concepts related to the instructional needs of the students.**

This may include the description of an appropriate instructional sequence, including the use of appropriate activities and materials or examples, to teach a basic concept or skill. In describing an instructional sequence, ensure that all appropriate components have been addressed and arranged in the most logical order. Select educational activities, materials, and examples that will help to clarify the concept for the students, that are appropriate for the age level you are addressing, and that build understanding sequentially.

Test takers sometimes lose points by describing a jumble of activities lacking any sense of direction, although the individual activities might be appropriate. Be sure that you describe a genuine instructional sequence in which each successive activity builds better understanding.

7. **Reread your response to check that you have written what you thought you wrote.**

   Frequently, sentences are left unfinished or clarifying information is omitted. Check for correct use and spelling of all educational terms.

The General Scoring Guide for the *Education of Young Children* (0021) Test

The following guide provides the framework for scoring the constructed-response questions on the *Education of Young Children* test.

The responses are scored according to the scoring guide below, on a scale of 0 to 3.

<u>Score</u>	<u>Comment</u>
3	The response is successful in the following ways:
	▪ All parts of the exercise are responded to fully and accurately.
	▪ The response demonstrates a strong knowledge of subject matter relevant to the question.
	▪ The response is insightful, developmentally appropriate, and substantive.
	▪ The suggestions are connected, effective, and developmentally appropriate.
2	The response demonstrates some understanding of the topic but may show unevenness in the evidence in one or more of the following ways:
	▪ Some parts of the question are not answered appropriately.
	▪ The response may demonstrate only superficial knowledge of the subject matter relevant to the question.
	▪ The response is only somewhat developmentally appropriate.
	▪ The explanation is appropriate, but not as closely connected as in a score of 3.
1	The response is seriously flawed in one or more of the following ways:
	▪ Most parts of the question are not answered adequately.
	▪ The response demonstrates weak understanding of the subject matter.
	▪ The description is sketchy, inappropriate, or trivial.
	▪ The explanation is ineffective, loosely connected, partial, or missing.

0   The response is represented in one or more of the following ways:

  - Blank, off-topic, or totally incorrect response

  - Does nothing more than restate the question or some phrases from the question

  - Demonstrates severely limited understanding of the topic

Question-Specific Scoring Guides

After a question is developed, three or four knowledgeable experts develop ideas for "model answers." These model answers are used to develop a "Question-Specific Scoring Guide" that creates a list of specific examples that would receive various scores. This list contains examples of various answers, not all possible answers. These question-specific scoring guides, which are based on model answers, provide the basis for choosing the papers that serve as the benchmarks and sample papers used for training the scorers at the scoring session. During the scoring sessions, specific examples can be added to the scoring guide, and papers can be added as samples for future readings.

Understanding what the questions are asking

You cannot write a successful response to a question unless you thoroughly understand the question. Often test takers jump into their written response without taking enough time to analyze exactly what the question is asking, how many different parts of the question need to be addressed, and how the information in accompanying charts or tables needs to be addressed. The time you invest in making sure you understand what the question is asking will very likely pay off in a better performance, as long as you budget your time and do not spend a large proportion of the available time just reading the question.

A sample question

To illustrate the importance of understanding the question before you begin writing, let's start with a sample question:

  Part A: The parents of your first-grade students will be coming into your room for parent/teacher conferences. List FOUR materials that your parents would see in a learning center that foster geometry and spatial skills.

  Part B: Basing your response on principles of child development and learning, explain how each of these chosen materials will foster a child's geometry and spatial skills.

Key components of the question

  - There are *two parts* to the question.

  - Both parts must be answered.

  - The response must be developmentally appropriate for first-grade students.

  - Part A must list four materials that foster geometry and spatial skills.

  - Part B must be based on principles of child development and learning and explain how each of the four chosen materials will foster a child's geometry and spatial skills. An explanation must be included; it is not sufficient to merely indicate or list the information.

Organizing your response

Successful responses start with successful planning, either with an outline or with another form of notes. By planning your response, you greatly decrease the chances that you will forget to answer any part of the question. You increase the chances of creating a well-organized response, which is something the scorers look for. Your note-taking space also gives you a place to jot down thoughts whenever you think of them—for example, when you have an idea about one part of the question when you are writing your response to another part. Like taking time to make sure you understand what the question is asking, planning your response is time well invested, although you must keep track of the time so that you leave sufficient time to write your response.

To illustrate a possible strategy for planning a response, let us focus again on the sample question introduced in the previous section. We analyzed the question and found that it asked for a two-part response. You might begin by jotting down those parts on your notes page, leaving space under each. This will ensure that you address each part when you begin writing.

Sample notes—main parts to be answered

Part A.	FOUR materials
Part B.	Explain chosen materials

Sample notes—ideas under each main part

You then might quickly fill out the main ideas you want to address in each part, like this:

Part A.	List FOUR materials that foster geometry and spatial skills
Part B.	Explain how these chosen materials will foster geometry and spatial skills

These are key requirements that the scorers will look for:

- Answer all parts of the question.
- Give reasons for your answers.
- Demonstrate subject-specific knowledge in your answer.
- Refer to the data in the stimulus.

Now look at your notes and add any ideas that would address these characteristics. Notice the additions that have been made on the next page.

Sample notes, with added ideas

Part A.	List FOUR materials that foster geometry and spatial skills - Materials must be appropriate for first-grade students - Materials must be appropriate for a learning center - Response may be in the form of a list
Part B.	Explain how these chosen materials will foster geometry and spatial skills - Response must be based on principles of child development and learning - Response must be in the form of an explanation

You have now created the skeleton of your written response.

Writing your response

Now the important step of writing your response begins. The scorers will not consider your notes when they score your paper, so it is crucial that you integrate all the important ideas from your notes into your actual response.

Some test takers believe that every written response on a Praxis™ test has to be in formal essay form—that is, with an introductory paragraph, then paragraphs with the response to the question, then a concluding paragraph. This is the case for very few Praxis tests (e.g., *English* and *Writing*). The *Education of Young Children* test does **not** require formal essays, so you should use techniques that allow you to communicate information efficiently and clearly. For example, you can use bulleted or numbered lists, or a chart, or a combination of essay and chart.

Returning to our sample question, note below how the outline of the response to the first part of the question can become the final written response. Since the question states "List FOUR materials," it is appropriate for you to respond with a list.

Part A:	The parents of my first-grade students will be coming into my room for parent/teacher conferences. In order to assist the parents in understanding what the children are learning in our program, I will show them a learning center for mathematics. The following four materials are in the learning center and foster geometry and spatial skills: • attribute blocks • geoboards • tangrams • base 10 blocks

While a list may be appropriate for responding to Part A of the question, Part B asks for an explanation. A sample response to Part B, based on the outline created in the previous section, is shown below.

Part B: Principles of child development and learning support the knowledge that children learn best by being actively involved in the process. They need to be "hands-on" in the learning process, which means that the children must be able to touch the materials and manipulate them in order to fully understand their properties. In the early stages of learning, children learn best visually; they need to see things, rather than just hear about them. This is why we have learning centers, rather than lecture halls, in our first grade classroom. The materials that were chosen are hands-on and visual representations of mathematical concepts and will foster geometry and spatial skills.

The attribute blocks will foster learning of both geometry and spatial skills because the blocks are in geometric shapes and show different attributes that identify spatial differences (size, thickness). The blocks may also be used to show the attributes of color, allowing for children to identify the red hexagon or blue rhombus. Children can sort the blocks by shape (e.g., all triangles), thereby reinforcing geometric concepts, or arrange the blocks by size (e.g., large circles and small circles), thereby reinforcing spatial concepts.

Geoboards allow the student to make a geometric shape (e.g., a rectangle) and then reconstruct it spatially by dividing the shape into two or more parts. Rather than recognizing the shape, as with the attribute blocks, the student will construct the shape with the geoboard and rubber bands.

Tangrams focus on geometric shapes and are important in encouraging students to identify patterns among the shapes, as well as identifying likenesses and differences. Tangrams are similar to attribute blocks in that the student will identify the shape rather than construct it. Tangrams can be arranged in various configurations to make other shapes and figures, thereby reinforcing spatial relationships.

Base 10 blocks take a basic geometric shape (the cube, which is 1 square centimeter) and allow students to combine cubes to form longs (10 cubes in a row), flats (10 longs side by side, or 100 cubes), and large cubes (10 flats stacked, which equals 100 longs, or 1000 cubes). Arranging the cubes in different configurations allows the student to visually understand the spatial relationship among the different combinations (10 cubes equal one long, one cube is one-tenth of a long). Base 10 blocks may be utilized in numerous ways. A student could display 34 separate cubes or 3 longs and 4 cubes to show the same number, using a visual representation to reinforce a numerical concept and the spatial concept that 34 separate cubes takes up the same space as 3 longs and 4 cubes. A student could also count out 71 cubes into one pile and 17 cubes into another pile to understand place value and the spatial concept that the same numbers (7 and 1) have different meaning and take up different space according to the arrangement of the digits (71 or 17).

Overall, these four materials (attribute blocks, geoboards, tangrams, and base 10 blocks) reinforce the principles of child development and learning that a child learns best by being actively involved. They are excellent learning tools that foster geometry and spatial skills by providing the child with visual representations of abstract mathematical concepts.

Whatever format you select, what matters most is that your answer is thorough, complete, and detailed. You need to be certain that you do the following:

- Answer all parts of the question.
- Give reasons for your answers.
- Demonstrate subject-specific knowledge in your answer.
- Refer to the data in the stimulus.

The Scoring Process

As you build your skills in writing answers to constructed-response questions, it is important to keep in mind the process used to score the tests. If you understand the process by which experts award your scores, you will have a better context in which to think about your strategies for success.

The scoring session

After each test administration, all test books are returned to ETS. The multiple-choice answer sheets are scored with the use of scanning machines. *Education of Young Children* booklets are bundled and sent to the location of the scoring session.

The scoring session usually takes place two weeks after the test administration and lasts for two, three, or four days, depending on how many tests need to be scored. Each session is led by a "chief scorer," a highly qualified preschool or elementary school teacher who has many years' experience scoring test questions. All of the remaining scorers are also experienced preschool and elementary school teachers and early childhood education teacher-educators. New scorers are thoroughly trained to understand and use all of the scoring materials. Experienced scorers are retrained, with the same approach, at each session and help to train the new scorers. Experienced scorers provide continuity with past sessions, while new scorers provide fresh perspectives. New scorers ensure that the pool of scorers remains large enough to cover the test's needs throughout the year.

At a typical scoring session, eight to twelve scorers are seated at three or four tables, with any new scorers distributed equally across all tables. One of the scoring leaders, the chief scorer, or a table leader sits at each table. The "chief scorer" is the person who has overall authority over the scoring session and plays a variety of key roles in training and in ensuring consistent and fair scores. Table leaders assist the chief scorer with these responsibilities.

Preparing to train the scorers

Training scorers is a rigorous process, and it is designed to ensure that each response gets a score that is consistent both with the scores given to other papers and with the overall scoring philosophy and criteria established for the test when it was first designed.

The chief scorer first takes the scorers through a review of the "General Scoring Guide," which contains the overall criteria, stated in general terms, for awarding a score. The chief scorer also reviews and discusses— and, when there are new test questions, makes additions to—the question-specific scoring guides, which apply the rubrics in the general guide to each specific question on the test. The question-specific guides are not intended to cover every possible response the scorers will see. Rather, they are designed to give enough examples to guide the scorers in making accurate judgments about the variety of answers they will encounter.

To begin identifying appropriate training materials for an individual question, the chief scorer first reads through many responses from the bundles of responses to get a sense of the range of the responses. The chief scorer then chooses a set of "benchmarks," typically selecting two responses at each score level for each question. These benchmarks serve as representative examples of the kind of response that meets the criteria of each score level and are the foundation for score standards throughout the session.

The chief scorer then chooses a set of test taker responses to serve as "sample" papers. These sample papers represent the wide variety of possible responses that the scorers might see. The sample papers will serve as the basis for practice scoring at the scoring session, so that the scorers can rehearse how they will apply the scoring criteria before they begin.

The process of choosing a set of benchmark responses and a set of sample responses is followed systematically for each new question to be scored at the session. After the chief scorer is done with selections and discussions, the chosen sets are photocopied and inserted into the scorers' folders for use in future sessions.

Training the scorers

For each question, the training session proceeds in the same way:

1. All scorers review the "General Scoring Guide" and the question-specific scoring guides.

2. All scorers carefully read through the question.

3. The leaders guide the scorers through the set of benchmark responses, explaining in detail why each response received the score it did. Scorers are encouraged to ask questions and share their perspectives. All of the scorers are trained together to ensure uniformity in the application of the scoring criteria.

4. Scorers then practice on the set of samples chosen by the leaders. The leaders poll the scorers on what scores they would award and then lead a discussion to ensure that there is consensus about the scoring criteria and how they are to be applied.

5. When the leaders are confident that the scorers will apply the criteria consistently and accurately, the actual scoring begins.

Quality-control processes

There are a number of procedures that are designed to ensure that the accuracy of scoring is maintained during the scoring session and to ensure that each response receives as many points as the scoring criteria allow. The test books, for example, are designed so that any personal or specific information about the examinee, such as name and test center location, are never seen by the scorers. Additionally, each response is scored twice, with the first scorer's decision hidden from the second scorer. If the two scores for a paper are the same or differ by only one point, the scoring for that paper is considered complete, and the test taker will be awarded the sum of the two scores. If the two scores differ by more than one point, the response is scored by the chief scorer and the response's score is revised accordingly.

Another way of maintaining scoring accuracy is through "back-reading." Throughout the session, the chief scorer checks a random sample of scores awarded by scorers. If the leader finds that a scorer is not applying the scoring criteria appropriately, that scorer is given more training and his/her scores are checked. The chief scorer also back-reads all responses that received scores differing by more than one point to ensure that every appropriate point has been awarded.

Finally, the scoring session is designed so that a number of different scorers contribute to any single test taker's score. This minimizes the effects of a scorer who might score slightly more rigorously or generously than other scorers.

The entire scoring process—standardized benchmarks and samples, general and specific scoring guides, adjudication procedures, back-reading, scorer statistics, and rotation of exams to a variety of scorers—is applied consistently and systematically at every scoring session to ensure comparable scores for each administration and across all administrations of the test.

Chapter 6
Practice Test, *Education of Young Children*

Now that you have studied the content topics and have worked through strategies relating to multiple-choice and constructed-response questions, you should take the following practice test. You will probably find it helpful to simulate actual testing conditions. You can cut out and use the answer sheet provided if you wish.

Keep in mind that the test you take at an actual administration will have different questions and, depending on which test you take, may have a different format. The *Early Childhood Education* (0020) test consists of 120 multiple-choice questions, and the *Pre-Kindergarten Education* (0020) test consists of 103 multiple-choice questions—neither of these tests includes any constructed-response questions. If you plan to take one of these tests, you may choose to skip Part B of this practice test (the part that contains the constructed-response questions) and allow yourself only the 90 minutes that Part A requires. The *Education of Young Children* (0021) test consists of both multiple-choice and constructed-response questions, so if you plan to take the *Education of Young Children* test, you should complete both Part A and Part B of the practice test. Allow yourself about 150 minutes (two and one-half hours). Note that the actual *Education of Young Children* test contains only 60 multiple-choice questions, not the 90 included in this practice test. The proportion of practice questions in each content area is approximately the same as what you will find on the actual *Education of Young Children* test. You should not expect the percentage of questions you answer correctly in this practice test to be exactly the same as when you take the *Education of Young Children* test at an actual administration, since numerous factors affect a person's performance in any given testing situation.

When you have finished the practice questions, you can score your answers and read the explanations of the best answer choices in chapter 7. In chapter 8 you may see sample responses to the constructed-response questions, together with the scores they received and comments from the chief scorer.

TEST NAME:

Education of Young Children
Practice Questions

Time—150 minutes

Part A: 90 Multiple-Choice Questions

Part B: Constructed-Response Questions

(Note: At the official test administration of the *Early Childhood Education* test, there will be 120 questions with five answer choices for each question, and you will be allowed 120 minutes to complete the test. At the administration of the *Education of Young Children* test, there will be 60 multiple-choice questions and six constructed-response questions, and you will be allowed 120 minutes to complete the test. At the administration of the *Pre-Kindergarten Education* test, there will be 103 multiple-choice questions, and you will be allowed 120 minutes to complete the test.)

Answer Sheet C

PAGE 1

THE PRAXIS SERIES
Professional Assessments for Beginning Teachers®

DO NOT USE INK

Use only a pencil with soft black lead (No. 2 or HB) to complete this answer sheet.
Be sure to fill in completely the oval that corresponds to the proper letter or number.
Completely erase any errors or stray marks.

1. NAME

Enter your last name and first initial.
Omit spaces, hyphens, apostrophes, etc.

Last Name (first 6 letters)						F I
Ⓐ Ⓑ Ⓒ Ⓓ Ⓔ Ⓕ Ⓖ Ⓗ Ⓘ Ⓙ Ⓚ Ⓛ Ⓜ Ⓝ Ⓞ Ⓟ Ⓠ Ⓡ Ⓢ Ⓣ Ⓤ Ⓥ Ⓦ Ⓧ Ⓨ Ⓩ						

2.

YOUR NAME: _____
(Print)
Last Name (Family or Surname)   First Name (Given)   M. I.

MAILING ADDRESS: _____
(Print)
P.O. Box or Street Address   Apt. # (if any)

City   State or Province

Country   Zip or Postal Code

TELEPHONE NUMBER: (____) _____
Home   Business

SIGNATURE: _____   **TEST DATE:** _____

3. DATE OF BIRTH

Month	Day
Jan.	
Feb.	
Mar.	
April	
May	
June	
July	
Aug.	
Sept.	
Oct.	
Nov.	
Dec.	

Day ovals: ⓪ ① ② ③ ④ ⑤ ⑥ ⑦ ⑧ ⑨

4. SOCIAL SECURITY NUMBER

⓪ ① ② ③ ④ ⑤ ⑥ ⑦ ⑧ ⑨

5. CANDIDATE ID NUMBER

⓪ ① ② ③ ④ ⑤ ⑥ ⑦ ⑧ ⑨

6. TEST CENTER / REPORTING LOCATION

Center Number   Room Number

Center Name

City   State or Province

Country

7. TEST CODE / FORM CODE

⓪ ① ② ③ ④ ⑤ ⑥ ⑦ ⑧ ⑨

0
1

8. TEST BOOK SERIAL NUMBER

9. TEST FORM

10. TEST NAME

51055 • 08920 • TF71M500   Q2573-06
MH01159

I.N. 202974

1   2   3   4

CERTIFICATION STATEMENT: (Please write the following statement below. DO NOT PRINT.)

"I hereby agree to the conditions set forth in the *Registration Bulletin* and certify that I am the person whose name and address appear on this answer sheet."

_____

_____

_____

SIGNATURE: _____ DATE: _____ / _____ / _____

Month   Day   Year

BE SURE EACH MARK IS DARK AND COMPLETELY FILLS THE INTENDED SPACE AS ILLUSTRATED HERE: ● .

1 Ⓐ Ⓑ Ⓒ Ⓓ	41 Ⓐ Ⓑ Ⓒ Ⓓ	81 Ⓐ Ⓑ Ⓒ Ⓓ	121 Ⓐ Ⓑ Ⓒ Ⓓ
2 Ⓐ Ⓑ Ⓒ Ⓓ	42 Ⓐ Ⓑ Ⓒ Ⓓ	82 Ⓐ Ⓑ Ⓒ Ⓓ	122 Ⓐ Ⓑ Ⓒ Ⓓ
3 Ⓐ Ⓑ Ⓒ Ⓓ	43 Ⓐ Ⓑ Ⓒ Ⓓ	83 Ⓐ Ⓑ Ⓒ Ⓓ	123 Ⓐ Ⓑ Ⓒ Ⓓ
4 Ⓐ Ⓑ Ⓒ Ⓓ	44 Ⓐ Ⓑ Ⓒ Ⓓ	84 Ⓐ Ⓑ Ⓒ Ⓓ	124 Ⓐ Ⓑ Ⓒ Ⓓ
5 Ⓐ Ⓑ Ⓒ Ⓓ	45 Ⓐ Ⓑ Ⓒ Ⓓ	85 Ⓐ Ⓑ Ⓒ Ⓓ	125 Ⓐ Ⓑ Ⓒ Ⓓ
6 Ⓐ Ⓑ Ⓒ Ⓓ	46 Ⓐ Ⓑ Ⓒ Ⓓ	86 Ⓐ Ⓑ Ⓒ Ⓓ	126 Ⓐ Ⓑ Ⓒ Ⓓ
7 Ⓐ Ⓑ Ⓒ Ⓓ	47 Ⓐ Ⓑ Ⓒ Ⓓ	87 Ⓐ Ⓑ Ⓒ Ⓓ	127 Ⓐ Ⓑ Ⓒ Ⓓ
8 Ⓐ Ⓑ Ⓒ Ⓓ	48 Ⓐ Ⓑ Ⓒ Ⓓ	88 Ⓐ Ⓑ Ⓒ Ⓓ	128 Ⓐ Ⓑ Ⓒ Ⓓ
9 Ⓐ Ⓑ Ⓒ Ⓓ	49 Ⓐ Ⓑ Ⓒ Ⓓ	89 Ⓐ Ⓑ Ⓒ Ⓓ	129 Ⓐ Ⓑ Ⓒ Ⓓ
10 Ⓐ Ⓑ Ⓒ Ⓓ	50 Ⓐ Ⓑ Ⓒ Ⓓ	90 Ⓐ Ⓑ Ⓒ Ⓓ	130 Ⓐ Ⓑ Ⓒ Ⓓ
11 Ⓐ Ⓑ Ⓒ Ⓓ	51 Ⓐ Ⓑ Ⓒ Ⓓ	91 Ⓐ Ⓑ Ⓒ Ⓓ	131 Ⓐ Ⓑ Ⓒ Ⓓ
12 Ⓐ Ⓑ Ⓒ Ⓓ	52 Ⓐ Ⓑ Ⓒ Ⓓ	92 Ⓐ Ⓑ Ⓒ Ⓓ	132 Ⓐ Ⓑ Ⓒ Ⓓ
13 Ⓐ Ⓑ Ⓒ Ⓓ	53 Ⓐ Ⓑ Ⓒ Ⓓ	93 Ⓐ Ⓑ Ⓒ Ⓓ	133 Ⓐ Ⓑ Ⓒ Ⓓ
14 Ⓐ Ⓑ Ⓒ Ⓓ	54 Ⓐ Ⓑ Ⓒ Ⓓ	94 Ⓐ Ⓑ Ⓒ Ⓓ	134 Ⓐ Ⓑ Ⓒ Ⓓ
15 Ⓐ Ⓑ Ⓒ Ⓓ	55 Ⓐ Ⓑ Ⓒ Ⓓ	95 Ⓐ Ⓑ Ⓒ Ⓓ	135 Ⓐ Ⓑ Ⓒ Ⓓ
16 Ⓐ Ⓑ Ⓒ Ⓓ	56 Ⓐ Ⓑ Ⓒ Ⓓ	96 Ⓐ Ⓑ Ⓒ Ⓓ	136 Ⓐ Ⓑ Ⓒ Ⓓ
17 Ⓐ Ⓑ Ⓒ Ⓓ	57 Ⓐ Ⓑ Ⓒ Ⓓ	97 Ⓐ Ⓑ Ⓒ Ⓓ	137 Ⓐ Ⓑ Ⓒ Ⓓ
18 Ⓐ Ⓑ Ⓒ Ⓓ	58 Ⓐ Ⓑ Ⓒ Ⓓ	98 Ⓐ Ⓑ Ⓒ Ⓓ	138 Ⓐ Ⓑ Ⓒ Ⓓ
19 Ⓐ Ⓑ Ⓒ Ⓓ	59 Ⓐ Ⓑ Ⓒ Ⓓ	99 Ⓐ Ⓑ Ⓒ Ⓓ	139 Ⓐ Ⓑ Ⓒ Ⓓ
20 Ⓐ Ⓑ Ⓒ Ⓓ	60 Ⓐ Ⓑ Ⓒ Ⓓ	100 Ⓐ Ⓑ Ⓒ Ⓓ	140 Ⓐ Ⓑ Ⓒ Ⓓ
21 Ⓐ Ⓑ Ⓒ Ⓓ	61 Ⓐ Ⓑ Ⓒ Ⓓ	101 Ⓐ Ⓑ Ⓒ Ⓓ	141 Ⓐ Ⓑ Ⓒ Ⓓ
22 Ⓐ Ⓑ Ⓒ Ⓓ	62 Ⓐ Ⓑ Ⓒ Ⓓ	102 Ⓐ Ⓑ Ⓒ Ⓓ	142 Ⓐ Ⓑ Ⓒ Ⓓ
23 Ⓐ Ⓑ Ⓒ Ⓓ	63 Ⓐ Ⓑ Ⓒ Ⓓ	103 Ⓐ Ⓑ Ⓒ Ⓓ	143 Ⓐ Ⓑ Ⓒ Ⓓ
24 Ⓐ Ⓑ Ⓒ Ⓓ	64 Ⓐ Ⓑ Ⓒ Ⓓ	104 Ⓐ Ⓑ Ⓒ Ⓓ	144 Ⓐ Ⓑ Ⓒ Ⓓ
25 Ⓐ Ⓑ Ⓒ Ⓓ	65 Ⓐ Ⓑ Ⓒ Ⓓ	105 Ⓐ Ⓑ Ⓒ Ⓓ	145 Ⓐ Ⓑ Ⓒ Ⓓ
26 Ⓐ Ⓑ Ⓒ Ⓓ	66 Ⓐ Ⓑ Ⓒ Ⓓ	106 Ⓐ Ⓑ Ⓒ Ⓓ	146 Ⓐ Ⓑ Ⓒ Ⓓ
27 Ⓐ Ⓑ Ⓒ Ⓓ	67 Ⓐ Ⓑ Ⓒ Ⓓ	107 Ⓐ Ⓑ Ⓒ Ⓓ	147 Ⓐ Ⓑ Ⓒ Ⓓ
28 Ⓐ Ⓑ Ⓒ Ⓓ	68 Ⓐ Ⓑ Ⓒ Ⓓ	108 Ⓐ Ⓑ Ⓒ Ⓓ	148 Ⓐ Ⓑ Ⓒ Ⓓ
29 Ⓐ Ⓑ Ⓒ Ⓓ	69 Ⓐ Ⓑ Ⓒ Ⓓ	109 Ⓐ Ⓑ Ⓒ Ⓓ	149 Ⓐ Ⓑ Ⓒ Ⓓ
30 Ⓐ Ⓑ Ⓒ Ⓓ	70 Ⓐ Ⓑ Ⓒ Ⓓ	110 Ⓐ Ⓑ Ⓒ Ⓓ	150 Ⓐ Ⓑ Ⓒ Ⓓ
31 Ⓐ Ⓑ Ⓒ Ⓓ	71 Ⓐ Ⓑ Ⓒ Ⓓ	111 Ⓐ Ⓑ Ⓒ Ⓓ	151 Ⓐ Ⓑ Ⓒ Ⓓ
32 Ⓐ Ⓑ Ⓒ Ⓓ	72 Ⓐ Ⓑ Ⓒ Ⓓ	112 Ⓐ Ⓑ Ⓒ Ⓓ	152 Ⓐ Ⓑ Ⓒ Ⓓ
33 Ⓐ Ⓑ Ⓒ Ⓓ	73 Ⓐ Ⓑ Ⓒ Ⓓ	113 Ⓐ Ⓑ Ⓒ Ⓓ	153 Ⓐ Ⓑ Ⓒ Ⓓ
34 Ⓐ Ⓑ Ⓒ Ⓓ	74 Ⓐ Ⓑ Ⓒ Ⓓ	114 Ⓐ Ⓑ Ⓒ Ⓓ	154 Ⓐ Ⓑ Ⓒ Ⓓ
35 Ⓐ Ⓑ Ⓒ Ⓓ	75 Ⓐ Ⓑ Ⓒ Ⓓ	115 Ⓐ Ⓑ Ⓒ Ⓓ	155 Ⓐ Ⓑ Ⓒ Ⓓ
36 Ⓐ Ⓑ Ⓒ Ⓓ	76 Ⓐ Ⓑ Ⓒ Ⓓ	116 Ⓐ Ⓑ Ⓒ Ⓓ	156 Ⓐ Ⓑ Ⓒ Ⓓ
37 Ⓐ Ⓑ Ⓒ Ⓓ	77 Ⓐ Ⓑ Ⓒ Ⓓ	117 Ⓐ Ⓑ Ⓒ Ⓓ	157 Ⓐ Ⓑ Ⓒ Ⓓ
38 Ⓐ Ⓑ Ⓒ Ⓓ	78 Ⓐ Ⓑ Ⓒ Ⓓ	118 Ⓐ Ⓑ Ⓒ Ⓓ	158 Ⓐ Ⓑ Ⓒ Ⓓ
39 Ⓐ Ⓑ Ⓒ Ⓓ	79 Ⓐ Ⓑ Ⓒ Ⓓ	119 Ⓐ Ⓑ Ⓒ Ⓓ	159 Ⓐ Ⓑ Ⓒ Ⓓ
40 Ⓐ Ⓑ Ⓒ Ⓓ	80 Ⓐ Ⓑ Ⓒ Ⓓ	120 Ⓐ Ⓑ Ⓒ Ⓓ	160 Ⓐ Ⓑ Ⓒ Ⓓ

FOR ETS USE ONLY	R1	R2	R3	R4	R5	R6	R7	R8	TR	CS

Part A

90 Multiple-choice Questions
Suggested time—90 Minutes

1. Four 3-year-old boys and girls are playing with dolls on the floor. Each child is holding and grooming one doll without interacting with a nearby neighbor. Which of the following categories of play does this scenario describe?

   (A) Symbolic
   (B) Associative
   (C) Parallel
   (D) Cooperative

2. Children between the ages of 2 and 7 years lack the ability to perform certain mental operations. The ability to undo a problem mentally and go back to its beginning is one of them. Which of the following terms applies to this ability?

   (A) Conservation
   (B) Reversibility
   (C) Centration
   (D) One-to-one correspondence

3. Which type of act by a 3 year old is an outward manifestation of beginning symbolization?

   (A) Tracing shapes
   (B) Coloring in a coloring book
   (C) Scribbling with crayons
   (D) Gluing shapes on paper

4. Which of the following skills is LEAST likely to be performed by a 3 year old?

   (A) Galloping
   (B) Jumping
   (C) Skipping
   (D) Hopping

5. Jamie is a 3-year-old child who is beginning preschool soon. His mother is concerned because he usually cries and screams in unfamiliar places. He cries when taken for a haircut and to have his picture taken. Which of the following temperament dimensions is this behavior related to?

   (A) Activity level
   (B) Attention span
   (C) Distractibility
   (D) Adaptability

6. Ms. Levine is a preschool teacher who works with 4-year-old children. When planning activities to increase the children's social development, she bases her practice on Piaget's concept that a young child's moral development is influenced by egocentrism. Which of the following best describes an effect of egocentrism on the moral development of young children?

   (A) Inability to take another's perspective
   (B) Understanding another's point of view
   (C) Tendency to consider the fairness of a situation
   (D) Ability to understand intentions of an action

7. Ms. Lee, a second-grade teacher, notices that many of the children develop increased self-control and ability to delay gratification during the school year. She notices that some of the children begin to take some responsibility for their own learning. Ms. Lee would most likely have noticed an increase in which of the following types of locus of control?

   (A) External
   (B) Biological
   (C) Internal
   (D) Physical

8. Social cognition theorists propose that most of a child's learning comes from which of the following?

   (A) Modeling what the child sees and hears other people say and do
   (B) Repeating behaviors that are reinforced by others
   (C) Chemical and electrical changes that develop within the body
   (D) Repeating demonstrated behaviors that are common to all children

9. Which of the following activities is likely to help preschool students improve fine motor skills?

   (A) Walking across a balance beam that is only a few inches off the ground
   (B) Playing hopscotch on the blacktop and counting the squares as they hop
   (C) Running relay races in the school gym in teams of five students each
   (D) Creating different shapes with clay using cookie cutters and rolling pins

10. An early reader can be distinguished from an emergent reader in that an early reader

    (A) understands the difference between letters and words
    (B) detects the beginning sounds in spoken words
    (C) knows that print communicates information
    (D) self-corrects recognized errors when reading aloud

11. A second-grade reading teacher wants to assess a student's reading abilities. Which of the following questions would help the teacher assess the student's ability to activate schema?

    (A) Does the student connect the text to personal experiences?
    (B) Is the student able to recall plot elements and sequence events?
    (C) Can the student synthesize information by capturing the main ideas of the passage?
    (D) Is the student able to decode unfamiliar words?

12. Which of the following types of play is more common during middle-childhood years than during preschool years?

    (A) Onlooker
    (B) Solitary
    (C) Parallel
    (D) Cooperative

13. A 6-year-old student is asked to memorize a telephone number. The teacher encourages the student to repeat the number as a means of memorizing it. Which of the following memorization strategies is this an example of?

    (A) Association
    (B) Chunking
    (C) Rehearsal
    (D) Visual imaging

14. According to Piaget, children at the preoperational level can typically comprehend which of the following?

    (A) The height of an object
    (B) The height and width of an object
    (C) The height, width, and length of an object
    (D) The height, width, length, and surface area of an object

15. Which of the following is a teacher able to assess by administering a cloze test?

    (A) Students' ability to sound out unfamiliar words
    (B) Students' ability to define frequently used words
    (C) Students' ability to sequence events correctly
    (D) Students' ability to use syntactic and semantic clues in text

16. Which of the following process skills does a student mainly use when grouping objects by color, shape, or other attributes?

    (A) Classifying
    (B) Observing
    (C) Recording
    (D) Measuring

17. Mr. Kray sends the following note home to parents:

    > Dear Families:
    >
    > Please look around your home with your child and find words that your child can read. These may be words like <u>blue</u> on a blue crayon or <u>orange juice</u> on the juice container. Please have your child bring the items to school. Also, please have your child bring in an empty cereal box.
    >
    > Thanks,
    >
    > Mr. Kray

    Which of the following is the most likely purpose of this exercise?

    (A) To reinforce students' exposure to environmental print
    (B) To initiate correspondence with families
    (C) To begin exercises in syllabification with students
    (D) To have the students create a collage of print and paper in class

18. Eighteen-month-old Mathias learns the colors yellow, red, and blue through playing with brightly colored plastic blocks with his mother. One day Mathias and his teacher are sharing a book. Mathias points at a picture of a brightly colored sun and says, "Yellow." Which of the following skills is Mathias demonstrating?

    (A) Decentering
    (B) Generalizing
    (C) Conventional reasoning
    (D) Accommodation

19. Which two of the following words have an unvoiced consonant as their first letter?

    I.   Bean
    II. Foot
    III. Kick
    IV. Near

    (A) I and II
    (B) I and III
    (C) II and III
    (D) II and IV

20. Which of the following describes the correct ascending order of Maslow's hierarchy of lifelong needs?

    (A) Safety, self-actualization, belonging, esteem, physiological
    (B) Physiological, belonging, safety, self-actualization, esteem
    (C) Physiological, safety, belonging, esteem, self-actualization
    (D) Safety, physiological, belonging, esteem, self-actualization

21. Ms. Craig asks her students to write the word *sailboat*. Levi spells the word PKLLEEP. At which of the following levels is Levi spelling?

    (A) Pre-phonemic
    (B) Phonemic
    (C) Transitional
    (D) Conventional

22. Which of the following is NOT a characteristic of the guided reading approach?

    (A) It enables students to participate in story prediction.
    (B) It increases the time students spend reading.
    (C) It provides a clear scope and sequence of reading skills.
    (D) It promotes reading fluency.

23. A 3-year-old child says to her parents, "Look, the sun followed us home." The mother asks the child, "What do you think the sun is?" The child replies, "He is a big happy face. He smiles."

    Which of the following is this child demonstrating?

    (A) Transductive reasoning
    (B) Animistic thinking
    (C) Horizontal decalage
    (D) Egocentrism

24. A school playground is next to a very busy street. A 4-year-old child, Pedro, opens the playground gate and is about to cross the road in order to go after a ball. The teacher, on the far side of the playground, looks up and sees the child about to go into the road.

    According to research about childhood development, which of the following approaches should the teacher use to get the child's attention and deter him from entering the busy street?

    (A) Shout, "Pedro, don't cross the street!"
    (B) Blow a whistle and shout, "Don't cross the street!"
    (C) Say in a normal voice, "Pedro, stop."
    (D) Shout, "Pedro, Don't!"

25. Kevin, a kindergartner, has difficulty writing with a pencil. He grasps it so tightly that its point often breaks off as he writes. Which of the following statements about kindergartners' development would account for Kevin's problem?

    (A) Kindergartners' muscles need to be constantly active.
    (B) Kindergartners tend to focus on small details when writing letters.
    (C) A 5 year old is not developmentally ready to write with a pencil.
    (D) Development of small muscles is ongoing in the primary grades.

26. A father approaches a teacher because he is concerned that his preschool-age son expresses a great fondness for playing with dolls and kitchen toys in the classroom. Which of the following responses by the teacher would be most appropriate in this situation?

    (A) Offering to ask the student to consider playing with other toys because his current choices are upsetting to his father
    (B) Explaining to the father that the toys children play with often cross traditional gender lines and that gender roles become more defined as children age
    (C) Explaining to the father that many of the other students in the class choose to play with toys that do not conform to stereotypical views of male and female gender roles
    (D) Offering to consult the school guidance counselor if any further aberrant behavior is observed

27. A kindergartner whose primary caregivers do not speak any English exhibits delayed expressive English-language development. Which of the following is an appropriate action for the teacher to take?

    (A) Seeking the help of a translator to translate key classroom information for the child
    (B) Sending home with the child an hour's worth of English audio practice each day
    (C) Encouraging the child to become immersed in social activities with peers
    (D) Asking the parents to use whatever words of English they know to help the child recover the language deficit

28. Michelle is a 3-year-old child who will be starting school soon at the Head Start program in her town. She has lived in several foster homes and has a history of significant neglect during infancy. According to Bowlby's attachment theory, which of the following areas would be a core concern?

    (A) Speaking
    (B) Cognitive activities
    (C) Healthy eating habits
    (D) Social relationships

29.

    ▪ Activity level
    ▪ Threshold of responsiveness
    ▪ Biological rhythms
    ▪ Attention span and persistence
    ▪ Intensity of reaction
    ▪ Quality of mood

    The traits above are often assessed to determine which of the following about a child?

    (A) Motivation
    (B) Temperament
    (C) Social development
    (D) Cognitive development

30. Which of the following conditions is NOT a likely trigger for an asthma attack in a young child?

    (A) Furry or feathered pets
    (B) Strenuous activity
    (C) Child-to-child contact
    (D) Cigarette smoke

31. At the beginning of the school year, a kindergarten student begins complaining to a parent about stomachaches and headaches and some insomnia. Which of the following is the most likely cause of the child's discomfort?

    (A) Agoraphobia
    (B) Separation-anxiety disorder
    (C) Attention deficit disorder
    (D) Procrastination

32. Which of the following is the single most effective way of preventing the spread of communicable diseases, such as the common cold, in pre-K and kindergarten classrooms?

    (A) Spraying diluted bleach on tabletop surfaces and on commonly handled toys
    (B) Spraying disinfectant into the air before the students arrive
    (C) Frequent hand washing by the teacher and children
    (D) Providing fruits rich in vitamin C at snack time

33. Which of the following is NOT true with regard to the disease chicken pox?

    (A) Individuals with compromised immune systems and pregnant women should be isolated from individuals with chicken pox.
    (B) Epidemics of chicken pox typically arise in the late winter and early spring.
    (C) The contagious period for chicken pox begins two days before the skin blisters appear and lasts until all the blisters are crusted over.
    (D) A person cannot contract chicken pox after receiving the chicken pox shot.

34. Sandra is a student in Mr. Kelly's kindergarten class. She recently began wearing a patch over her right eye in response to a diagnosis of amblyopia. Which of the following would best describe her need for the eye patch?

    (A) Preventing the spread of infection
    (B) Increasing the vision in her left eye
    (C) Increasing the vision in her right eye
    (D) Protecting her eye after surgery

35. A teacher notices that a 7-year-old boy, Jamal, cannot sit still or finish his assignments. He constantly drums on his desk and does not pay attention during class. The teacher's goal is to find ways to help him control his behavior and focus on schoolwork. According to research, all of the following would improve Jamal's focus and behavior EXCEPT

   (A) dividing tasks into manageable parts and giving meaningful praise when it is deserved
   (B) establishing a reward system with incentive goals to encourage positive behavior
   (C) instituting consistent penalty actions when Jamal fails to finish assignments or displays inattention during class
   (D) allowing Jamal to move around and/or to stand while doing his schoolwork

36. Mr. Johnson notices that students in his classroom tend to bring in very unhealthy snacks for snack time. Which of the following is an appropriate way for Mr. Johnson to respond to the students' eating habits?

   (A) Planning a lesson or activity to identify healthy foods
   (B) Eliminating snack time from the routine
   (C) Allowing only students with healthy foods to eat snacks
   (D) Changing the routine to include exercise after snack time

37. Kate is a 7-year-old child who attends a second-grade classroom where she is given many opportunities for success in learning new skills. She finds pleasure in being productive. According to Eric Erikson's psychosocial stages, Kate is demonstrating a positive outcome for which of the following developmental crises?

   (A) Trust vs. mistrust
   (B) Industry vs. inferiority
   (C) Autonomy vs. doubt
   (D) Identity vs. role confusion

38. According to Piaget, during which of the following stages of cognitive development does the child begin to understand the concept of object permanence?

   (A) Preoperational
   (B) Sensorimotor
   (C) Concrete operational
   (D) Formal operational

39. All of the following are true of the Reggio Emilia approach EXCEPT:

   (A) Documentation of student work is an important element of the approach.
   (B) The presence of the school workshop (atelier) makes it possible for students to express themselves and learn through different media.
   (C) The approach follows a structured and spiraling curriculum.
   (D) Reggio Emilia educators believe that children co-construct knowledge and that the small group is the ideal learning situation.

40. How can the teacher keep the students engaged and provide opportunity for repetition and revision when the students are participating in whole-group instruction?

   (A) By setting clear and concise objectives
   (B) By pacing instruction appropriately
   (C) By providing wait time after questioning
   (D) By checking for understanding intermittently

41. Which of the following theorists developed the idea of the "zone of proximal development" (ZPD) to refer to the distance between what a child can complete independently and what the child can accomplish with the help of a teacher or caregiver?

   (A) Jean Piaget
   (B) Albert Bandura
   (C) Lev Vygotsky
   (D) Erik Erikson

42. According to Howard Gardner's theory of multiple intelligences, a student with high kinesthetic intelligence and low interpersonal and linguistic intelligences would be most likely to learn science concepts in which of the following ways?

    (A) Discussing them with other students
    (B) Finding ways to act them out
    (C) Writing about them
    (D) Reading about them

43. During circle time, Mr. Lennox plays an activity record that instructs the children to jump, hop, skip, crawl, and throw a ball. Which of the following is Mr. Lennox attempting to foster through these exercises?

    (A) Development of coordination and fine motor skills
    (B) Development of social skills and habituation
    (C) Understanding of patterning and one-to-one correspondence
    (D) Understanding of how to follow directions and development of gross motor skills

44. Which of the following statements about components of emergent literacy are true?

    I. Literacy development begins before a child enters kindergarten.
    II. Reading and writing are two distinct skills that develop independently of each other.
    III. Children's early unconventional attempts at writing (i.e., scribbles and other markings) may be viewed as expressions of early writing.

    (A) II only
    (B) I and II only
    (C) I and III only
    (D) II and III only

45. Which of the following statements best describes the moral reasoning of a typical student in kindergarten?

    (A) The student will begin adopting his or her parents' moral standards and seek to be thought of as a "good girl" or "good boy."
    (B) The student will understand that moral judgments are based on understanding one's social duty.
    (C) The student will focus on advancing his or her own self-interest by trying to maximize rewards and minimize punishments.
    (D) The student will begin to understand that some values are more important than the law.

46. Which of the following should a teacher do if a 3-year-old student in the class bites another student?

    (A) Speak to the parents of the biting child and suggest that the child receive counseling.
    (B) Express disapproval immediately and remove the biting child from the social situation.
    (C) Keep both students physically separated in future classes.
    (D) Downplay attention to the incident since biting is fairly common in preschool.

47. Which of the following early childhood programs was launched in 1965 in an effort to give economically disadvantaged children advance preparation for the intellectual and social challenges of elementary school?

    (A) High/Scope
    (B) Montessori
    (C) Bank Street model
    (D) Project Head Start

48.

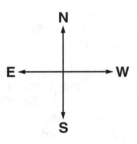

After a geography lesson on cardinal points, nearly one-half of the students in a first-grade class label a compass as shown above. Which of the following is the LEAST developmentally appropriate strategy to help these students?

(A) Placing an "E" sticker on the students' right hands and a "W" sticker on their left hands

(B) Having students use hand-held compasses to find their way around the school

(C) Teaching students a song that names each direction as they move clockwise around a compass on the floor

(D) Assigning students to locate and list ten cities in the Eastern Hemisphere and ten in the Western Hemisphere

49. A kindergarten teacher holds an orange up in front of an open container filled with water. She asks her group of students, "Do you think this orange will float if we peel off the rind?" The teacher peels the orange and then asks a student to put it into the water. The students watch the experiment. After the demonstration, the teacher writes the information on a chart on the wall. Which of the following science skills is the teacher reinforcing by using this activity?

(A) Using simple graphs and recognizing patterns

(B) Clarifying questions and interpreting data

(C) Making a hypothesis and recording observations

(D) Categorizing and using simple tools to extend their observations

50. All of the following guidelines for arranging a typical second-grade classroom would be both developmentally appropriate and academically effective EXCEPT

(A) maintaining a quiet, carpeted area of books and media materials

(B) furnishing the room with child-sized desks, chairs, and tabletops

(C) creating storage and organizational spaces that allows students to store and retrieve materials

(D) utilizing all wall space, doors, bulletin boards, windows, and lights for print and decoration

51. Which of the following is an example of incidental learning occurring in the classroom?

(A) Students in Mr. Pearl's class receive assignments for various tasks, such as watering class plants, collecting and distributing materials, and sharpening pencils.

(B) Ms. Chen asks her students to imagine what their lives would be like if television had never been invented. She then assigns students to work in groups to write a play about life without television.

(C) Ms. Rayne asks her third graders to describe the ways in which they show their respect for the community.

(D) Six-year-old Joshua observes 6-year-old Raj being rewarded for saying "please" in order to get something he wants from the teacher, Mr. Green.

52. A teacher's daily schedule includes the use of board games and group games that children can choose to play in small groups. The teacher encourages the children to design games where the children make up specific rules and then teach the games to other children. Which of the following social and emotional skills would most likely be promoted through these activities?

    (A)   Solitary and parallel play
    (B)   Dependence and compliance
    (C)   Autonomy and cooperation
    (D)   Role-playing and fantasy

53. Ms. Ruiz is a kindergarten teacher who is concerned about classroom management during free play, when conflicts among the children occur frequently. Which of the following should Ms. Ruiz do first when conflicts arise?

    (A)   Remove the children involved in the conflict from the play center.
    (B)   Observe the issues of the conflict and determine an intervention.
    (C)   End play time early and substitute a teacher-directed activity.
    (D)   Interve immediately and solve the children's conflict.

54. Mr. Davis is a first-grade teacher in an inclusion classroom. One of the children in the classroom is often ignored by peers and is uninvolved in most of the social activities. Which of the following would be the most important strategy for increasing the social status of the child within the classroom?

    (A)   Depriving the class of privileges when the child is not included in play
    (B)   Punishing any child who purposely rejects another child
    (C)   Allowing the children to work things out themselves
    (D)   Demonstrating that the child is worthy of the teacher's attention

55. Which of the following math manipulatives would be most appropriate for a second-grade teacher to use when students explore place value?

    (A)   Base-ten blocks
    (B)   Pennies
    (C)   Geoboards
    (D)   Six-sided number cube

56. How can a spiraling curriculum be used most valuably?

    (A)   To support connections across disciplines by focusing learning experiences on a central theme
    (B)   To encourage students to learn in cooperation with other students at different levels
    (C)   To enable teachers to teach the same group of students each year in a given discipline
    (D)   To foster a broad understanding of a concept by revisiting it at each grade level

57. A class of seventeen first-grade students attends an assembly on owls in the school auditorium. A nature explorer shows slides of owls and the wilderness habitats she has visited. After 30 minutes, several of the students begin to move around in their seats and make noise. Which of the following would provide the best explanation for the children's behavior?

    (A)   The children are bored by the subject matter.
    (B)   The children relate to owls only as fictional characters.
    (C)   The auditorium environment is foreign to the students.
    (D)   The students have been focusing for too long on the lecture.

58.

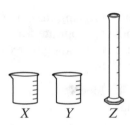

X   Y   Z

A teacher presents a young child with two glass beakers (X and Y) and a graduated cylinder (Z). Beakers X and Y are identical in size, and graduated cylinder Z is taller and thinner. The teacher pours the same amount of water into X and Y and asks the child if the two containers (beakers X and Y) have the same amount of water. The child responds, "Yes." Next the teacher pours the water from beaker Y into graduated cylinder Z and asks if the two containers (beakers Y and Z) have the same amount of water. The child responds, "No." When asked which one has more, the child points to graduated cylinder Z.

What is this experiment designed to determine about the child?

(A) The child's understanding of conservation
(B) The child's understanding of theory of mind
(C) The child's ability to categorize materials
(D) The child's ability to generalize

59. Mary insists that her father is a daddy only, not a son or a brother as well, because she sees her father only in the role he plays for her. This is an example of which of the following?

(A) Attachment
(B) Egocentrism
(C) Centration
(D) Ideation

60. A parent reads the picture book *Caps for Sale* to his 3-year-old son, who can identify colors. The father points to the illustration and says to the child, "Point to the monkey—not the one in the red hat, not the one in the blue hat, but the one in the green hat."

This reading-related task will help the

(A) child develop visual discrimination and an understanding of conversational patterns
(B) child relate the story to personal experiences and develop phonemic awareness
(C) child gain understanding of traditional story grammar and predictable characters
(D) parent conduct a miscue analysis

61. Which of the following is the best example of a behavioral objective in a social studies curriculum?

(A) By the end of the year, students will know the historical events and democratic values commemorated by national holidays.
(B) During the first month of school, students will learn the significance of the Pledge of Allegiance and patriotic songs.
(C) At the end of the lesson, students will be able to identify the school and their neighborhood on an aerial map of the county.
(D) By the end of the unit, students will gain appreciation for regional folk heroes and popular figures who have contributed to the cultural history of the United States of America.

62. Which of the following activities is most likely to help highly visual learners comprehend the key concepts in a chapter on the human skeletal system?

   (A) Taking careful notes when the teacher reviews the chapter
   (B) Rereading the chapter at home with more privacy
   (C) Discussing the key concepts with fellow students in a small group
   (D) Drawing a web diagram of the key concepts presented in the chapter

63. At the beginning of the school year, a first-grade teacher observes that a student is unable to use beginning and final consonants correctly while reading. Which of the following is most likely to help the student develop these skills?

   (A) Modeling words in context and teaching decoding skills
   (B) Showing a video of a popular children's story and stopping to discuss words that appear in the story
   (C) Pairing the student with another student who is able to use consonants correctly
   (D) Displaying pictures and corresponding printed words around the room

64. At the end of a second-grade reading unit, a teacher reads the following sentences in a student's response journal:

   > This is a long tail. Their onced was a sun. He worked in a coal mind. He was sooty. Then he found a garland. That is a red gem.

   This student needs help with which of the following?

   (A) Synonyms
   (B) Antonyms
   (C) Phonics
   (D) Homophones

65. A class has finished reading a novel. Which of the following actions by the teacher is most likely to foster continued interest in reading fiction?

   (A) Calling on students to answer questions about the story's theme and setting
   (B) Having small groups of students discuss what they liked and disliked about the story and why
   (C) Telling students that there will be a follow-up assignment to compare the story with other stories they have read
   (D) Asking students to prepare a graphic organizer that shows the relationship between story parts

66. As part of a language arts program, a first-grade teacher takes student on field trips, reads aloud from books frequently, and equips the classroom with pictures and prints. Which of the following student needs is met by all of these instructional practices?

   (A) Facilitated social adjustment
   (B) Expanded reading readiness
   (C) Increased motor development
   (D) Improved auditory ability

67. A teacher in a pre-K classroom does the following during circle time:

   - Draws students' attention to uppercase and lowercase letters in books and charts
   - Points to and reads words, labels, and letters
   - Shows children that people read print by moving left to right and top to bottom
   - Identifies features of a book, such as the title, the author, and the jacket

   Which of the following is the teacher trying to reinforce with these activities?

   (A) Sequence of story
   (B) Variety of genres
   (C) Concept of print
   (D) Decoding skills

68. How is Friedrich Froebel significant to the field of early childhood education?

(A) He developed the theory that children's intellectual development is primarily a function of developmental stages and time.

(B) He began a preschool program for disadvantaged children, ages 4 to 6, and demonstrated that well-designed instruction could accelerate cognitive skills.

(C) He formulated the first kindergarten system, in which the child engages in play activities called "occupations" with natural building blocks and other toys called "gifts."

(D) He developed a constructivist math approach in which he explained knowledge as being invented within the child and not passively absorbed from the environment.

69. A third-grade teacher is introducing cursive writing. The teacher tells her student to use the "Magic c," and the teacher draws the letter "c" to create the letter "q." Which strategy is the teacher employing with this approach?

(A) Showing students how to use a "tow line" to connect one letter in the alphabet to other letters

(B) Using a lowercase letter to show students how to write an uppercase letter

(C) Using repetition to help students master new letter forms

(D) Using one letter in the alphabet to help students learn to form other letters

70. Following a unit on sound, a second-grade teacher wants to evaluate student understanding of the concept that sound is produced by vibrations. Which of the following is an example of an authentic assessment that would serve that purpose?

(A) Students write journal entries describing what they have learned during the unit on sound.

(B) Students design and construct their own musical instruments, using materials the teacher provides.

(C) Students draw pictures showing all the things they can think of that make sound.

(D) Students complete a test in which they are asked to explain how sounds are made.

71. Which of the following mathematical skills would a teacher help a child develop using Unifix cubes?

(A) Adding numbers
(B) Identifying place value
(C) Recognizing shape
(D) Forming numbers

72. A preschool teacher has planned several demonstrations for his students. First he drops a ball lightly to the ground, and it bounces several inches. Next he throws the ball with more force toward the ground, causing the ball to bounce several feet. Then he lightly shakes a tambourine to produce a quiet sound, and finally he shakes it vigorously to produce a loud sound.

Which of the following early-childhood concepts about science might be the focus of this demonstration?

(A) Conservation
(B) Sequencing
(C) Simple machines
(D) Functional relationships

73. At a staff meeting, the principal asks the staff to list some strategies for reducing student stress and anxiety in the classroom. Of the following suggestions, which is NOT an appropriate technique?

    (A) Include physical activity each day.
    (B) Promote role-playing and self-expression in the classroom.
    (C) Suggest that students draw their feelings.
    (D) Encourage students to sit silently at their desks when agitated.

74. A teacher puts words onto cards and presents them to students in the following way:

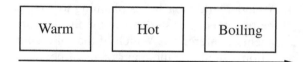

Which of the following graphic organizing tools is the teacher using to present information to the students?

    (A) A linear array
    (B) A Venn diagram
    (C) A semantic-feature grid
    (D) A word map

75. A third-grade student scores in the 43rd percentile on a standardized state test. Which of the following would be an accurate way for the teacher to report these results to the child's parents?

    (A) The child answered 43 percent of the test questions correctly.
    (B) The child has learned 43 percent of the third-grade content tested by the state.
    (C) The child performed better than 43 percent of third graders in the state.
    (D) The child completed 43 percent of the test.

76. The River Street School assesses all entering kindergarten children. According to NAEYC guidelines for initial assessment, how can this information be used most effectively?

    (A) To gather data for school comparisons
    (B) To identify children who need another year of preschool
    (C) To adjust curriculum and instruction
    (D) To diagnose children with disabilities

77. The parents of 3-year-old Patricia ask that she receive diagnostic screening because of her history of developmental delays. Which of the following describes the most appropriate activities for assessing Patricia's skills?

    (A) Identifying and pointing to pictures
    (B) Manipulating toys and real objects
    (C) Completing paper-and-pencil tasks
    (D) Answering oral questions

78. Ms. Polasky, the director of a preschool center for children ages 3 to 5, has provided in-service training for the teachers on the Work Sampling System developed by Meisels and his colleagues.

Which of the following best describes this type of assessment?

    (A) Curriculum embedded
    (B) Norm referenced
    (C) Criterion referenced
    (D) Developmental screening

79. Which of the following describes the most effective use of portfolios in discussing a child's progress with parents?

    (A) Comparing the child's work samples to the work of others in the class
    (B) Comparing the child's work samples to a norm group
    (C) Summarizing how closely the child's work resembles the teacher's examples
    (D) Summarizing the child's growth through the use of a variety of earlier and later work samples

80. The third-grade class at Carver Elementary School is developing plays based on their favorite stories. They are working in small groups to create props and scenery as well as to rewrite the stories into dramas. Their teacher will use this activity to assess the students' reading comprehension and writing skills.

Which of the following best describes this type of assessment?

(A) Norm referenced
(B) Formal
(C) Authentic
(D) Traditional

81. The teachers at the Third Street Elementary School are given the state curriculum standards for the grade they teach. They are asked to document the children's growth and progress in their classrooms so that they can plan an effective curriculum.

Which of the following would be the most effective method of documenting growth and progress towards the curriculum standards for individual children and for each class as a group?

(A) Norm-referenced tests
(B) Developmental checklists
(C) Report-card grades
(D) End-of-chapter tests

82. Brandon is a 4-year-old child who was referred for a multidisciplinary evaluation by his teacher because of speech/language delays. Which of the following settings would the speech/language specialist find most beneficial for observing Brandon's level of language functioning?

(A) Formal assessment session
(B) Structured speech session
(C) Classroom during free-play activities
(D) Classroom during teacher-directed activities

83. The teachers at the White Mountain Elementary School have been using performance-based instructional methods. The teachers often assess the students by using rating scales based on specific criteria. The teachers develop narratives that describe varying levels of proficiency for the tasks being rated.

Which of the following best describes this type of assessment tool?

(A) Running record
(B) Anecdotal notes
(C) Rubrics
(D) Portfolio

84. A kindergarten teacher is planning to meet with the parents of her students at the fall parent-teacher conferences. Which of the following actions should be the main focus of her discussions with the parents?

(A) Explaining how the parents can best work with their child at home
(B) Discussing the parents' responsibilities in the child's learning
(C) Detailing the child's weak areas and giving suggestions for improvement
(D) Discussing the child's growth and needs in a positive manner

85. Mr. Lakewood is working on report cards for his second-grade students. He considers the information he has gathered from portfolios, checklists, tests, and anecdotal records on each student.

Which of the following would be the most comprehensive method for him to use in reporting the students' progress?

(A) Letter grades
(B) Number grades
(C) Skills checklists
(D) Descriptive narratives

86. A class is about to participate in a hands-on science experiment. One student uses a wheelchair and cannot reach the table where the lab has been set up. What would be the most effective action for the teacher to take to ensure this student's full participation?

    (A) Giving the physically challenged student a work sheet that covers the same information the rest of the class is learning
    (B) Placing the physically challenged student in a location that makes it easy to observe the experiment from a wheelchair
    (C) Setting up an additional lab area in the classroom that is within reach of the physically challenged student
    (D) Sending the physically challenged student to another classroom until the experiment is completed

87. Some parents of students in a second-grade classroom have not visited their children's classroom or attended any school functions. Which of the following is the LEAST effective way to promote parental classroom visitation?

    (A) Mailing out a sign-up sheet for parent-teacher conferences and asking parents to choose two dates during the school year
    (B) Holding a monthly parent meeting and sending invitations to parents asking that they attend
    (C) Calling the parents to discuss the possibility that they will visit the classroom
    (D) Sending home with the students a weekly newsletter reporting on the many enjoyable classroom activities that parents are invited to participate in

88. At kindergarten orientation, one of the teachers tells parents to label children's personal items, such as clothing, lunch boxes, and backpacks, by putting labels inside the items.

    Which of the following would best explain this placement of the labels?

    (A) To prevent strangers from having access to the children's first name
    (B) To prevent damage to the outside of the items
    (C) To prevent the children from knowing who the items belong to
    (D) To prevent the ink on the labels from running

89. All of the following are appropriate when talking to parents about their children's misbehavior EXCEPT

    (A) communicating expectations about classroom behavior
    (B) anticipating success in a plan for encouraging recommended behavior
    (C) describing how the child resembles and differs from other students in the classroom
    (D) using objective language to discuss the child's actions

90. Which of the following are appropriate duties for the paraprofessional in the classroom?

    I. Changing a student's behavioral modification plan and reporting the results of those changes to the teacher
    II. Helping a student who is attempting to run a program on a classroom computer
    III. Providing initial instruction to a student who is attempting multiplication
    IV. Organizing materials for daily instruction

    (A) I and II
    (B) I and III
    (C) II and III
    (D) II and IV

Part B

6 Constructed-response Questions
(Suggested time—60 minutes)

General Directions for Questions 61-66*: There are six questions in this section. Each question counts equally towards your score. Write your responses in the Response Book.

Suggested Approach for Questions 61-66: Read through the question before you begin responding. Then take a minute or two to make notes and organize your response. Since each question counts equally towards your score, you may want to spend about the same amount of time on each question.

Question 61

Part A: The parents of your kindergarten students will be coming into your room for parent/teacher conferences. List FOUR materials that the parents would see in a learning center that will promote visual and auditory skills related to reading.

Part B: Based on principles of child development and learning, explain how each of these chosen materials will foster a child's visual and auditory skills related to reading.

Question 62

Part A: You are encouraging the parents of your first-grade class to play a more active role in helping their children develop an appreciation of literature. Describe in detail TWO effective forms of communication that you would use to help parents understand the importance of an appreciation of literature.

Part B: What are TWO ways in which parents can take a proactive role in helping their children develop an appreciation of literature?

Question 63

You are planning an integrated unit on weather for the diverse learners in your kindergarten class.

Part A: Describe ONE developmentally appropriate, weather-related activity that integrates the following disciplines:

- science
- language arts
- math

Part B: Discuss the conceptual understanding that the activity will address in each content area.

---

* On the actual *Education for Young Children* test, these questions are always numbered 61 through 66, because there are 60 multiple-choice questions.

Question 64

STUDENT ASSIGNMENT: Add these problems. Show your work.

$34 + 9 =$ $67 + 18 =$ $35 + 17 =$

$$\begin{array}{r} 34 \\ + 9 \\ \hline 313 \end{array} \qquad \begin{array}{r} 67 \\ + 18 \\ \hline 715 \end{array} \qquad \begin{array}{r} 35 \\ + 17 \\ \hline 412 \end{array}$$

Part A: The children in a second-grade class are completing a math assignment. Above is a sample of a student's work. Discuss TWO aspects of mathematics development that are evident in the student's work.

Part B: Based on the mathematics skills identified in Part A, describe TWO developmentally appropriate instructional strategies you might use to advance this child's mathematical skills.

Question 65

You are the preschool teacher of 4-year-old Roberta. One of Roberta's parents comes to pick her up after school and drive her home. This is the first time you have observed the parent with slurred speech and clumsy movements. You suspect that this parent has been drinking.

Part A: Based on practice that is ethical as well as professionally and legally prudent, what are your responsibilities to Roberta and her family as a teacher?

Part B: List THREE resources that you could use to help you to learn how best to handle the issues specific to this situation. Describe the information each resource could provide.

Question 66

Dylan is a child in your second-grade class who has a physical handicap that requires the use of a wheelchair.

Part A: Describe TWO appropriate adaptations or accommodations that would help Dylan continue to learn.

Part B: Explain how each adaptation or accommodation described in Part A could benefit Dylan.

Chapter 7

Right Answers and Explanations for the
Multiple-Choice Questions

Right Answers

Now that you have answered all of the practice questions, you can check your work. Compare your answers to the multiple-choice questions with the correct answers in the table below.

Question Number	Correct Answer	Content Category	Question Number	Correct Answer	Content Category
1	C	Growth, Development, and Learning of Young Children	23	B	Growth, Development, and Learning of Young Children
2	B	Growth, Development, and Learning of Young Children	24	C	Growth, Development, and Learning of Young Children
3	C	Growth, Development, and Learning of Young Children	25	D	Growth, Development, and Learning of Young Children
4	C	Growth, Development, and Learning of Young Children	26	B	Growth, Development, and Learning of Young Children
5	D	Growth, Development, and Learning of Young Children	27	C	Growth, Development, and Learning of Young Children
6	A	Growth, Development, and Learning of Young Children	28	D	Factors Influencing Individual Growth and Development
7	C	Growth, Development, and Learning of Young Children	29	B	Factors Influencing Individual Growth and Development
8	A	Growth, Development, and Learning of Young Children	30	C	Factors Influencing Individual Growth and Development
9	D	Growth, Development, and Learning of Young Children	31	B	Factors Influencing Individual Growth and Development
10	D	Growth, Development, and Learning of Young Children	32	C	Factors Influencing Individual Growth and Development
11	A	Growth, Development, and Learning of Young Children	33	D	Factors Influencing Individual Growth and Development
12	D	Growth, Development, and Learning of Young Children	34	B	Factors Influencing Individual Growth and Development
13	C	Growth, Development, and Learning of Young Children	35	C	Factors Influencing Individual Growth and Development
14	A	Growth, Development, and Learning of Young Children	36	A	Factors Influencing Individual Growth and Development
15	D	Growth, Development, and Learning of Young Children	37	B	Applications of Developmental and Curriculum Theory
16	A	Growth, Development, and Learning of Young Children	38	B	Applications of Developmental and Curriculum Theory
17	A	Growth, Development, and Learning of Young Children	39	C	Applications of Developmental and Curriculum Theory
18	B	Growth, Development, and Learning of Young Children	40	D	Applications of Developmental and Curriculum Theory
19	C	Growth, Development, and Learning of Young Children	41	C	Applications of Developmental and Curriculum Theory
20	C	Growth, Development, and Learning of Young Children	42	B	Applications of Developmental and Curriculum Theory
21	A	Growth, Development, and Learning of Young Children	43	D	Applications of Developmental and Curriculum Theory
22	C	Growth, Development, and Learning of Young Children	44	C	Applications of Developmental and Curriculum Theory

Question Number	Correct Answer	Content Category	Question Number	Correct Answer	Content Category
45	C	Applications of Developmental and Curriculum Theory	75	C	Evaluating and Reporting Student Progress and the Effectiveness of Instruction
46	D	Applications of Developmental and Curriculum Theory	76	C	Evaluating and Reporting Student Progress and the Effectiveness of Instruction
47	D	Applications of Developmental and Curriculum Theory	77	B	Evaluating and Reporting Student Progress and the Effectiveness of Instruction
48	D	Planning and Implementing Curriculum	78	A	Evaluating and Reporting Student Progress and the Effectiveness of Instruction
49	C	Planning and Implementing Curriculum	79	D	Evaluating and Reporting Student Progress and the Effectiveness of Instruction
50	D	Planning and Implementing Curriculum	80	C	Evaluating and Reporting Student Progress and the Effectiveness of Instruction
51	D	Planning and Implementing Curriculum	81	B	Evaluating and Reporting Student Progress and the Effectiveness of Instruction
52	C	Planning and Implementing Curriculum	82	C	Evaluating and Reporting Student Progress and the Effectiveness of Instruction
53	B	Planning and Implementing Curriculum	83	C	Evaluating and Reporting Student Progress and the Effectiveness of Instruction
54	D	Planning and Implementing Curriculum	84	D	Evaluating and Reporting Student Progress and the Effectiveness of Instruction
55	A	Planning and Implementing Curriculum	85	D	Evaluating and Reporting Student Progress and the Effectiveness of Instruction
56	D	Planning and Implementing Curriculum	86	C	Understanding Professional and Legal Responsibilities
57	D	Planning and Implementing Curriculum	87	C	Understanding Professional and Legal Responsibilities
58	A	Planning and Implementing Curriculum	88	A	Understanding Professional and Legal Responsibilities
59	C	Planning and Implementing Curriculum	89	C	Understanding Professional and Legal Responsibilities
60	A	Planning and Implementing Curriculum	90	D	Understanding Professional and Legal Responsibilities
61	C	Planning and Implementing Curriculum			
62	D	Planning and Implementing Curriculum			
63	A	Planning and Implementing Curriculum			
64	D	Planning and Implementing Curriculum			
65	B	Planning and Implementing Curriculum			
66	B	Planning and Implementing Curriculum			
67	C	Planning and Implementing Curriculum			
68	C	Planning and Implementing Curriculum			
69	D	Planning and Implementing Curriculum			
70	B	Planning and Implementing Curriculum			
71	A	Planning and Implementing Curriculum			
72	D	Planning and Implementing Curriculum			
73	D	Planning and Implementing Curriculum			
74	A	Planning and Implementing Curriculum			

Explanations of Right Answers

1. This question asks you to apply your knowledge of play modes for young children. It describes a state of parallel play, in which children are playing separately from others but with similar toys or in a manner that mimics their neighbor's play. (C), therefore, is the correct answer.

2. During the preoperational and operational stages of development, children learn how to undo problems and retrace their steps, a mental process referred to as reversibility. (B), therefore, is the correct answer.

3. This question asks you to apply your knowledge of development involving symbolization, which is one of the processes by which children learn to construct knowledge for themselves. Scribbling uses rudimentary symbols to express or communicate feelings, objects, actions, ideas, words, and more. Therefore, (C) is the correct answer.

4. Of the four activities, skipping and galloping are the two most difficult skills listed. Of the two, skipping requires greater coordination and is least likely to be performed by a 3 year old. (C), therefore, is the correct answer.

5. This question tests your understanding of temperamental qualities, which are used to describe the characteristic ways that infants and children respond to their environment. Children and infants with good adaptability will become comfortable in new situations and when involved with new activities. Children and infants with poor adaptability will cry and become upset in new situations and over extended periods of time. Therefore, (D) is the correct answer.

6. This question asks you to demonstrate your knowledge of Piaget's theory of moral development. Piaget describes the influence of egocentrism on the moral development of a child. One influence of egocentric thought is that the child is unable to consider his or her own view and someone else's view at the same time, or the inability to take another's perspective. Therefore, (A) is the correct answer.

7. This question tests your knowledge of the concept of locus of control. There are two types, internal and external. People with internal locus of control tend to take responsibility for their actions and have good self-management skills. People with external locus of control tend to blame circumstances for their mistakes and feel their successes are due to luck. Developmentally, infants and children become increasingly more capable of controlling events in their lives. The locus of control then becomes more internal. Therefore, (C) is the correct answer.

8. This question tests your knowledge of the cognitive social learning theory of Albert Bandura. This theory suggests that through observational learning (also called "modeling") one learns the behavior of others and then possibly adopts that behavior oneself. Therefore, the correct answer is (A).

9. While all of the activities are appropriate to the preschool classroom, the exercises in (A), (B), and (C) focus on developing gross motor skills. By working with clay and using simple tools, the child is developing fine motor skills. (D), therefore, is the correct answer.

10. Answer choices (A), (B), and (C) are all significant milestones in students' early literacy development. However, a more advanced student (at the emergent level) is reading aloud and self-correcting errors. (D), therefore, is the correct answer.

11. Connecting text to personal experience is a strategy that indicates the student is activating prior knowledge or schema when reading. For example, a child may pick up a science-fiction book and, being familiar with the genre, may expect to read about aliens in the book. (A), therefore, is the correct answer.

12. During the preschool years, a child is most likely to be observed engaged in parallel, onlooker, and solitary play. With greater maturity, the child will begin to participate more actively in games with peers. Therefore the correct answer is (D).

13. The correct answer is (C). The child is using repetition as a means of reinforcing the information. The other answer choices are different strategies for storing information in memory.

14. According to Piaget, children at the preoperational level can consider only one dimension at a time, such as the height or the width of an object. At the concrete operational level, children begin to understand the interaction of the two dimensions, height and width, and at the formal operations level, the child can understand the interaction of two or more variables. (A), therefore, is the correct answer.

15. A cloze test allows students to use their knowledge of word order (syntax) and sentence meaning (semantics) to predict and supply appropriate words in passages such as the one below:

    The very hungry boy went to the _____ .
    There he purchased a very large _____ .

    The correct answer, therefore, is (D).

16. The ability to classify an object by an attribute it shares with other objects is an important milestone in early childhood development. Although the child is doing some observation, the child is mainly classifying. The child is not measuring, and there is no indication that the child is recording the event. The correct answer, therefore, is (A).

17. This question tests your knowledge of environmental print, a fundamental concept in the teaching of reading. Children initially encounter written language within their social and cultural worlds in the form of street signs and labels on everyday packaging. The correct answer, therefore, is (A).

18. There is no indication that the child is focusing on more than one aspect of the picture, which is referred to as "decentering" (A). The child is not demonstrating conventional reasoning, (C), nor accommodating information, (D). He is showing he can transfer, or *generalize,* knowledge from one situation to another. Mathias recognizes the color yellow not only on plastic blocks, but also in paper books. (B), therefore, is the correct answer.

19. Voiced consonants, such as the /b/ in *bean* or the /n/ in *near,* are pronounced with a vibration from the vocal cords. Some other voiced consonants are /m/, /z/, and /l/. Unvoiced consonants, such as the /f/ in *foot* or the /k/ in *kick,* are pronounced entirely with the breath and without a vibration from the vocal cords. Some other unvoiced consonants are /p/, /s/, and /t/. The correct answer, therefore, is (C).

20. The human needs in Maslow's system range from the most basic physiological needs (e.g., food, shelter) to the realization of self-actualization, which is at the top of the chart. Therefore the correct answer is (C).

21. At the pre-phonemic stage, students know some letters and may begin experimenting with letters, but sound-symbol correspondence is absent. The correct answer, therefore, is (A).

22. The correct answer is (C). Because students routinely problem solve with new texts independently, the new skills are not learned or reinforced in a predetermined, sequenced manner.

23. Animistic thinking commonly occurs during the preoperational period. Children believe that inanimate objects, because they move or appear to move, are alive. The correct answer, therefore, is (B).

24. Research has proven that children's ability to process verbal commands is somewhat unsophisticated at this age. For young children, shouting the directions may elicit the opposite reaction. Additionally, the compound structure of the commands in (A) and (B) consists of two ideas: "don't" (the negating idea) and "cross the street" (positive action). This creates confusion for a child who is trying to process the command. Using one word, "stop," at a lower volume has been found to be much more effective. The correct answer, therefore, is (C).

25. Fine motor skills lag behind gross motor skills and develop throughout early and middle childhood. This ongoing development explains the common situation of a primary student who has difficulty manipulating a writing implement. As musculature develops and the child gains control over it, the level of difficulty diminishes. The correct answer, therefore, is (D).

26. Children typically explore their environment during their preschool years, and often this play crosses stereotypically gender-appropriate expectations. Research suggests that by age 5 and 6 children will have well-formed ideas (and prejudices) about gender-specific activities. (B), therefore, is the correct answer.

27. Research has shown that when children are at kindergarten age, the language skills that are most important to them and the easiest for them to develop in the classroom are social language skills—those learned on the playground and from peer interactions. Therefore the correct answer is (C).

28. This question tests your knowledge of attachment theory. The pattern of the infant's attachment to its primary caregiver is the basis for future social relationships. A child who suffers from neglect and deprivation during infancy is at risk for later difficulties in establishing social relationships. Therefore, (D) is the correct answer.

29. This question tests your understanding of the basic traits that make up the personality of a young child. Even at birth, several of these traits can be observed in children and are often known to remain constant over a lifetime. These traits are illustrations of a child's temperament, so the correct answer is (B).

30. Asthma episodes in students can be sudden and life-threatening. The conditions named are all possible causes of asthma attacks except for contagion by another student. The disease is noncommunicable. Therefore, (C) is the correct answer.

31. In class, children can show symptoms of stress, including fearfulness, whininess, and crying behaviors. These stress responses can be intensified when children are separated from guardians. Therefore the correct answer is (B).

32. This question tests your knowledge of infection control in the school environment. Young children, as well as school staff, should be encouraged to wash hands frequently to remove or destroy disease-causing germs transmitted by contaminated hands. Therefore the correct answer is (C).

33. This question tests your knowledge about a common childhood illness. (A), (B), and (C) are all true of chicken pox. The chicken pox vaccine prevents illness in 70 percent to 90 percent of those who receive it. Those who *do* develop chicken pox after vaccination have much milder symptoms with fewer skin blisters. Therefore, (D) is the correct answer.

34. This question tests your knowledge of amblyopia, a common vision problem of young children. Amblyopia, or "lazy eye," is a condition in which one eye becomes stronger and the image in the other eye may be ignored by the brain. It is very important for physicians to diagnose and correct this condition in early childhood since the vision in the weaker eye may become permanently impaired. One method to correct the condition is to cover the stronger eye with a patch so that the brain is forced to use the weaker eye, which will often become stronger. Therefore, (B) is the correct answer.

35. Answer choices (A), (B), and (D) are actions that are likely to help Jamal become a more confident and motivated learner. (C) is the correct answer for this question. Punitive actions are likely to frustrate Jamal further and will not serve as a motivating factor, nor will they focus his attention on learning.

36. As children develop, it is important for them to learn and to practice healthy eating habits. Because children may not receive adequate guidance in healthy eating at home, it is important for teachers to be prepared to address students' health and nutrition at school. (A), therefore, is therefore the correct answer.

37. This question asks you to demonstrate your knowledge of Erikson's psychosocial stages of development. A 7-year-old child falls into stage 4: Elementary and Middle School Years, when the crisis is Industry *vs.* Inferiority. The positive outcome is a sense of competence in learning new skills. The negative outcome would be a sense of inferiority if unable to find success in learning new skills. Therefore, (B) is the correct answer.

38. This question tests your knowledge of the stages in Jean Piaget's theory of cognitive development. The correct answer is (B). During the first two years of life, children accomplish the understanding that objects continue to exist even when they cannot be seen, heard, or touched.

39. The question tests your knowledge of the Reggio Emilia approach. This approach typically features a school workshop in which an art teacher supports students as they use different materials to discover and express their interests. Additionally, the teachers believe in documenting student work, student conversations, and student advancements to help guide instruction. Small-group learning and social learning are foundations of the approach. However, the approach does not dictate a structured curriculum. Therefore, the correct answer is (C).

40. While all four of these options are good teaching practices, only choice (D) provides opportunities to review, repeat, and revise the material in the lesson. Periodically checking student understanding during whole-group instruction also tends to keep students alert.

41. The "zone of proximal development" is Lev Vygotsky's term for the range of what a child can do, from independent activities to those that require a caregiver's support. The correct answer, therefore, is (C).

42. Kinesthetic learners are most likely to learn from acting out the concepts being taught. Discussing, writing, and reading are approaches that are not likely to be as successful with kinesthetic learners. The correct answer, therefore, is (B).

43. The correct answer is (D). The students are developing their gross motor skills with the exercises. The instructions direct the students to follow the motions; therefore, the students are following directions. No indication is given that the students are coordinating the movements or developing fine motor skills. The students are not learning social skills, nor are they really being habituated to an environment. Specific activities would have to be noted that would indicate patterning and one-to-one correspondence.

44. This question tests your knowledge of aspects of emergent literacy. Of the three statements, I and III are principles accepted by early childhood educators. The correct answer, therefore, is (C).

45. This question tests your knowledge of Kohlberg's stages of moral development. At age 5, the child is typically still in stage 1, known as the preconventional stage of moral development. This stage is characterized by an emphasis on literal obedience to rules and authority and avoiding punishment. The correct answer is therefore (C).

46. Ignoring the behavior, (D), would not be appropriate. Biting is a serious matter, even at this age, so the teacher must address the issue of biting promptly in order to extinguish the behavior. Mere separation, (C), will not accomplish this goal. (A), counseling, is an extreme reaction to the incident. (B) addresses the problem at once and is the correct answer.

47. The correct answer is (D). Project Head Start is a federally funded program that was started in 1965 to meet the needs of economically disadvantaged students in the United States.

48. (D) is the correct answer. The assignment is too abstract for students of this age, who would not have a good concept of hemispheres. All the other activities are more appropriate for these students, since each one has a concrete task to encourage learning.

49. While all of the options are science-related skills, in this particular activity students are asked to suggest a hypothesis (that the peeled orange will float or sink) and observe the teacher model recording the information. The correct answer, therefore, is (C).

50. Classrooms should be aesthetically pleasing, comfortable, and geared toward the learning goals of the curriculum. The decorating and furnishing plan described in (D), however, is cluttered and may be overstimulating, defeating the objectives of a good learning environment. (D), therefore, is the correct answer.

51. (A), (B), and (C) are all appropriate teacher-initiated activities for an early-elementary class. Only (D) is an example of incidental learning, and therefore it is the correct answer. According to Bandura's theory of incidental learning, Joshua is recognizing that Raj's behavior is being rewarded, and Joshua may begin modeling this behavior himself.

52. The correct answer is (C). Through this activity the teacher is promoting the children's autonomy by giving the children authentic tasks and inviting the children to teach and share their games with peers.

53. Unstructured playtime offers students the opportunity to learn social skills, such as manners and fair play, and to negotiate independent boundaries for themselves and peers. Conflicts will inevitably arise during free play, and part of the teacher's role is to help children understand factors contributing to conflict. The correct answer, therefore, is (B).

54. (D) is the correct answer. The teacher can serve as an effective role model by indicating through words and actions that every person in the class deserves respect and should be valued equally. The other choices are less likely to facilitate a change in attitude.

55. While (B), (C), and (D) are manipulatives that can be used in the classroom to teach counting, shapes, and probability, only (A) will help students learn about place value. Therefore, (A) is the correct answer.

56. In a spiraling curriculum, the same concept is revisited as students develop cognitively during their the elementary years. The theory behind a spiraling curriculum is that skills and concepts deepen at each grade level as understanding is deepened and broadened. The correct answer, therefore, is (D).

57. The best explanation for the children's behavior is (D). Research indicates that most 6-year-old children can focus for about ten minutes. After this they need to process information in a different way.

58. The correct answer is (A). The beaker test is a well-known Piagetian test to determine whether a child can think operationally. A child who answers "No," as the one is this study does, is not able to understand that an object has specific, consistent attributes, such as volume, despite superficial changes.

59. Centration is focusing, or centering, of attention on one characteristic to the exclusion of all others. This child can focus only on her father's parental role, not his role as a son or brother. The correct answer, therefore, is (C).

60. This question asks you to identify the discrete skills that are emphasized during one particular moment in a shared reading experience. Since the child is not reading aloud, and this is not a testing situation, (D) would not be an appropriate choice. There is no real indication that the child is relating the story to personal experience, nor does this task help the child understand predictable characters or story grammar. However, looking for and pointing to specific items in a picture helps a child develop visual discrimination, and the complex sentence structure the father uses to guide the child's action exposes the child to intricate conversational sentence patterns. Therefore, (A) is the correct answer.

61. While all of these activities may go on in elementary school—and some of these goals may be met to a greater or lesser extent depending upon the age and development of the children—only (C) is written in terms of what a student will be able to do at the end of the lesson. The correct answer, therefore, is (C).

62. Teachers should be familiar with several methods of instruction, as well as the theories behind those methods, in order to adapt their teaching to accommodate the variety of learning styles present in a classroom of students. Graphic organizers, web diagrams, and illustrations all help visual learners, because they organize the material to be learned using a format that is easily accessible to these students. (D), therefore, is the correct answer.

63. Choices (B) and (D) may be appropriate for building interest in reading and enhancing reading readiness. (C) might be appropriate for practicing new skills. Only (A) combines teaching of the needed skills with meaningful contexts in which to use them. The correct answer, therefore, is (A).

64. In the scenario presented here, the student has confused the word "sun" with the desired word "son." He has made several of these types of errors, which are known as homophone errors. (D) is the correct answer.

65. In this question, the teacher might have chosen any one of these activities to follow up the reading of the novel. However, discussion in class about what students liked and disliked about the story is the most likely of the choices to foster continued interest in reading fiction. Therefore, (B) is the correct answer.

66. Although these activities have several possible benefits for students as part of a language arts program, they are all designed to expand readiness for reading. (B), therefore, is the correct answer.

67. The teacher is sharing experiences with students that will help them understand that text carries meaning. Therefore, (C) is the correct answer.

68. Friedrich Froebel, the German educationalist, developed special educational materials (such as shaped wooden bricks and balls, known as "gifts") to help introduce children to physical concepts. He went on to formulate the kindergarten system. The correct answer, therefore, is (C).

69. In the lesson, the teacher is showing students how to use certain letter forms as the basis for other alphabet letters. The correct answer, therefore, is (D).

70. In authentic assessment, teachers directly examine student performance on tasks that require students to apply content knowledge from a particular unit and use processes and practices that are relevant to the particular discipline they are studying. The correct answer is (B). By having students design their own musical instruments, the teacher can gain insight into the skills and content knowledge the students have acquired.

71. Unifix cubes are interlocking plastic cubes that are most commonly used to help primary students learn to add and subtract small numbers. Therefore the correct answer is (A).

72. The correct answer is (D). By showing the students that the harder the ball is thrown, the higher the ball will bounce, the teacher is helping students understand the functional relationship between the force of the ball being thrown and the height it will reach. Likewise, the teacher is showing the students that the volume of sound from the tambourine is functionally related to the force with which the tambourine is shaken.

73. A teacher should have some knowledge of how to alleviate stress in the classroom. Often, asking students to sit silently further exacerbates their stress level. The correct answer, therefore, is (D). The other choices have been proven to alleviate stress in the classroom.

74. The correct answer is (A). A linear array can arrange words that have gradient meanings, such as *good, better,* and *best.* It helps students expand their vocabularies and see relationships between words more concretely.

75. When a child takes a norm-referenced test, the student's score is usually reported as a percentile. The percentile indicates the student's performance on the test relative to other test takers at the student's grade level. A student who scores in the 43rd percentile on a standardized test has performed better than 43 percent of other test takers at that grade level. The correct answer, therefore, is (C).

76. This question tests your knowledge of initial assessment of young children. According to NAEYC guidelines, initial assessment information should be used for adjusting the curriculum and instruction according to what the children already know. It should not be used for tracking, labeling, or excluding children from programs. (C), therefore, is the correct answer.

77. This question tests your knowledge of diagnostic screening of young children. According to NAEYC guidelines, diagnostic screening should involve observing the child manipulate objects. The screening should not involve pencil-and-paper testing or use of conceptual materials such as pictures. (B), therefore, is the correct answer.

78. The Work Sampling System, developed by Meisels and his colleagues, is a curriculum-embedded assessment that assesses and documents children's skills through a variety of procedures on multiple occasions. The correct answer, therefore, is (A).

79. Portfolios are an important instrument for summarizing a child's growth and development in a way that parents can understand easily. By comparing the child's work to earlier samples, the teacher can determine the child's growth and identify the child's instructional needs. It is not advisable to use the portfolio to compare the child's work to teacher samples or the work of peers. Typical work samples are not based on norms. The correct answer, therefore, is (D).

80. Authentic assessment requires students to demonstrate knowledge by performing natural, or "authentic," tasks. Such tasks require students to apply knowledge and skills rather than just recall information. The correct answer, therefore, is (C).

81. Developmental checklists based on state or local standards can be an effective way to document growth and progress and to plan the curriculum based on the results. The checklists can be used observationally and can be based on a variety of indicators. Report-card grades and end-of-chapter tests do not give enough information to document growth and progress related to state standards. A norm-referenced test is given only once and does not effectively use multiple indicators to document growth and progress of individual students on specific standards. (B), therefore, is the correct answer.

82. This question tests your understanding of the importance of observation in the natural environment. The best setting for observing a child's speech/language functioning is in the classroom during free-play activities, when the child is engaged in activities of interest with peers. The level of functioning is difficult to assess accurately in isolated settings such as a testing or therapy session. Observation during teacher-directed activities is not likely to lead to accurate assessment. (C), therefore, is the correct answer.

83. A rubric is designed to facilitate objective assessment of performance on tasks or projects. Criteria are developed, together with narratives, to help teachers determine a student's level of proficiency in completing the task or project. The correct answer, therefore, is (C)

84. (D) is the correct answer. The purpose of parent-teacher conferences is to discuss the student's growth and needs. Teachers should set a positive tone in order to establish a collaborative working relationship with parents.

85. The correct answer is (D). This question tests your knowledge of how to report students' progress when information has been gathered by multiple methods, such as observation, anecdotal records, and portfolios. The most comprehensive method is to write descriptive narratives because these can address individual differences in motivation, approaches to tasks, interests, and other important information that has been gathered. Letter and number grades, and also checklists, provide condensed information and lose most of the richness of detail that has been gathered.

86. Teachers should be able to adjust their instructional methods to meet the special needs of their students. Setting up an additional lab area in the classroom that is within reach of the student in a wheelchair is an effective course of action. Additionally, if the experiment is to be performed by groups of students, the physically challenged student should be included in a group, and all members of the group should work in the wheelchair-accessible lab area. Therefore, (C) is the correct answer.

87. The correct answer is (C). Answer choices (A), (B), and (D) are appropriate actions for the teacher to take. In choices (B) and (D), the teacher is communicating with the parents in a nonthreatening manner, offering general invitations. In choice (C), the teacher calls with a specific inquiry, which is more likely to be resented. (Note that in planning conferences with parents, teachers must consider the possibility that lack of transportation or another factor may prevent some parents from visiting the school.)

88. This question tests your knowledge of child safety. An abductor may use a first name to engage the child and appear to know the child. For this reason, identifying information, especially the first name, should not be visible on children's personal items. (A), therefore, is the correct answer.

89. Parents often experience feelings of powerlessness and guilt when a teacher contacts them with the news that their child is misbehaving in the classroom. When speaking with parents, the teacher should focus on what is appropriate and inappropriate about their child's behavior. The behavior of other children is not relevant, so the teacher should avoid making comparisons between individual students. Therefore, (C) is the correct answer.

90. A paraprofessional should support student learning, but the paraprofessional should never provide initial instruction (III) or make independent decisions about the curriculum in relation to students (I). The correct answer, therefore, is (D).

Chapter 8

Sample Responses and How They Were Scored:
Constructed-Response Part of the *Education of Young
Children* Test

▶ ▶ ▶ ▶ ▶ ▶ ▶ ▶ ▶ ▶ ▶ ▶

This chapter presents actual sample responses to the questions in the practice test and explanations for the scores they received.

The General Scoring Guide used to score the questions is reprinted here for your convenience.

Score	Comment
3	The response is successful in the following ways:

- All parts of the exercise are responded to fully and accurately.
- The response demonstrates a strong knowledge of subject matter relevant to the question.
- The response is insightful, developmentally appropriate, and substantive.
- The suggestions are connected, effective, and developmentally appropriate.

2	The response demonstrates some understanding of the topic but may show unevenness in the evidence in one or more of the following ways:

- Some parts of the question are not answered appropriately.
- The response may demonstrate only superficial knowledge of the subject matter relevant to the question.
- The response is only somewhat developmentally appropriate.
- The explanation is appropriate, but not as closely connected as in a score of 3.

1	The response is seriously flawed in one or more of the following ways:

- Most parts of the question are not answered adequately.
- The response demonstrates weak understanding of the subject matter.
- The description is sketchy, inappropriate, or trivial.
- The explanation is ineffective, loosely connected, partial, or missing.

0	The response is represented in one or more of the following ways:

- Blank, off-topic, or totally incorrect response
- Does nothing more than restate the question or some phrases from the question
- Demonstrates severely limited understanding of the topic

Question 61

Part A:	The parents of your kindergarten students will be coming into your room for parent/teacher conferences. List FOUR materials that the parents would see in a learning center that will promote visual and auditory skills related to reading.
Part B:	Based on principles of child development and learning, explain how each of these chosen materials will foster a child's visual and auditory skills related to reading.

We will now look at four actual responses to Question 61 and see how the scoring guide above was used to rate each response.

Sample response that earned a score of 3

> There are many ways to introduce children to print and literature. The first would be books on casette with the books there for the kids to follow along. The children can listen and follow along and make inferences about how print works.
>
> The second material parents would find is a lot of envrionmental print. I would have everything labeled and I would have familar signs & symbols in my room as well. For example, a stop sign on the bathroom door for when it is occupied.
>
> A third venue would be the alphabet people. In a learning center I would have all the alphabet people there on the wall. I would also have a box of plastic letters for kids to experiment making words. I would have alphabet books with interesting pictures for the kids to select to read. This would allow them to make connections from letters to real-life items.
>
> A forth example would be a journal. It would begin simple with them drawing pictures and me writing out what they want to write. They would trace words. Then the next week copy below my writing. Then when they mastered that have them copy it from another source.

Scoring Commentary

Both parts of the exercise are responded to fully and accurately.

Both parts are responded to fully and accurately, with four materials listed—books on cassette, environmental print, alphabet people and books, journal writing—that parents would see in a learning center that will promote visual and auditory skills related to reading. Each mention of the material is accompanied by an explanation of how the materials will foster a child's visual and auditory skills related to reading.

The response demonstrates a strong knowledge of subject matter relevant to the question.

The selection of the materials and the explanation reflect a strong knowledge of reading skills. Both visual and auditory skills are represented in the choices. Printed text (books) will reinforce visual skills, while auditory aids (books on cassette) will assist auditory learners. In addition, the response includes reading (books, labels), as well as constructing written text with the alphabet people and journal writing.

Sample Responses to Question 61, continued

The response is insightful, developmentally appropriate, and substantive.

The choices are developmentally appropriate and reflect materials that should be provided for kindergarten students. It allows the children to manipulate materials (in the form of plastic letters), listen to tapes, draw illustrations, and view illustrated books—all activities that are developmentally appropriate for kindergarten students.

The suggestions are connected, effective, and developmentally appropriate.

All of the suggestions are connected to the identified goal. Each suggestion is effective and developmentally appropriate.

Sample response that earned a score of 2

A)   The learning center of my classroom is created to enhance the cognitive skills of my students. There will be a book case that contains picture and word books. I will also place my Big books in this area. There will also be a head phone system for the children to listen to stories & hear songs such as their ABC's. I will also place flash cards in the center for the children to visually view the information that we cover in class. This will help them learn to recognize the visual shape of letters & numbers. The children will be in a very neat & structured enviroment in the reading center.

I will allow them to work in groups and allow them to read to & with me. In doing this, I hope to open their cognitive skills up to a new level of learning.

Scoring Commentary

Some parts of the question are not answered appropriately.

While four materials may be identified for Part A (picture and word books, Big Books, headphone system, flashcards), the materials are not distinct, and therefore parts of Part A are not answered appropriately. It would have been more appropriate to select materials that were truly independent of each other and that would reinforce different aspects of the children's reading skills.

The response may demonstrate only superficial knowledge of subject matter relevant to the question.

Because the selection of the materials did not identify four distinct materials, the response demonstrates only superficial knowledge of reading skills and instruction. In Part B, the explanation refers to allowing the children "to visually view the information that we cover in class. This will help them learn to recognize the visual shape of letters & numbers." This explanation offers some reasoning concerning the material selection, but the rationale is not in-depth and reflects only superficial knowledge.

The response is only somewhat developmentally appropriate.

The response is somewhat developmentally appropriate. While the materials do allow for the children to view books that are appropriate for them and also allow for the children to listen to tapes, another developmentally appropriate selection, there is no provision of opportunities that would encourage the children to physically interact with the materials.

The explanation is appropriate, but not as closely connected as in a score of 3.

The explanation is provided and is appropriate but is not as well developed as an explanation receiving a score of 3. Additional information should be included concerning how the chosen materials will foster children's visual and auditory skills related to reading.

Sample response that earned a score of 1

> In my kindergarten class, the parents would see books throughout the room. There will be books in each area of the room that go along with that area. Also, I will have book shelves filled with books on the children's level. Near the bookshelves, I will have an area for the children to sit in a circle while I read to them. There will be a chair for me, and maybe a few beanbag chairs for the children. I will also have bulliten boards which display what books we are currently reading, and projects we have done that go along with that reading.
>
> Having books scattered in each area shows the children that reading (books) are important for every area of life. Reading is needed to help you to learn all things. The bookshelves are needed to encourage reading during free time. Giving the children opportunities to read, and many books to choose from, will encourage them to continue reading as a leisure activity throughout life. Doing projects related to their reading alows them to use their creativity, open up their minds, and apply their reading to their own lives.

Scoring Commentary

Most parts of the question are not answered adequately.

Part A mentions four choices of materials: books, bookshelves, chairs, and bulletin board. The choices are not appropriate and are not fully distinct from each other. The value of the bookshelves and chairs are related to the books that are being read. The bulletin boards are also valuable only in relation to the reading projects. The explanation is provided but does not help clarify why these materials were chosen. Most parts of the question are not answered adequately.

The response demonstrates weak understanding of the subject matter.

The response demonstrates a weak understanding of the subject matter due to the limited choice of materials and a failure to explain how the choices would foster visual and auditory skills. The explanation states, "Having books scattered in each area shows the children that reading (books) are important for every area of life. Reading is needed to help you to learn all things." However, this explanation does not indicate how the mere presence of books will show children the importance of reading. In fact, the opposite may be conveyed since having books "scattered in each area" may convey the message to the students that books are not valued.

Sample Responses to Question 61, continued

The description is sketchy, inappropriate, or trivial.

The description of the kindergarten room is sketchy and trivial. More emphasis is placed on the position and type of the chairs than on the material that will be read to the children. ("Near the bookshelves, I will have an area for the children to sit in a circle while I read to them. There will be a chair for me, and maybe a few beanbag chairs for the children.")

The explanation is ineffective, loosely connected, partial, or missing.

While some parts of the explanation contain the potential of conveying effective information, most of the explanations fail to explain fully the rationale for the materials that were chosen. For example, the response states, "Doing projects related to their reading alows them to use their creativity, open up their minds, and apply their reading to their own lives." However, this explanation fails to indicate *what* projects will be done and what materials will be needed to complete these projects. In addition, the explanation states, "The bookshelves are needed to encourage reading during free time" and "Giving the children opportunities to read, and many books to choose from, will encourage them to continue reading as a leisure activity throughout life." This explanation fails to clarify what opportunities will be given to the children to read, what books they will be allowed to choose, and how these opportunities will encourage the children to continue reading as a leisure activity throughout their lives.

Question 62

Part A:	You are encouraging the parents of your first-grade class to play a more active role in helping their children develop an appreciation of literature.
	Describe in detail TWO effective forms of communication that you would use to help parents understand the importance of an appreciation of literature.
Part B:	What are TWO ways in which parents can take a proactive role in helping their children develop an appreciation of literature?

The same 0–3 scoring guide used for Question 61 is applied to each part of this question.

We will now look at three samples and see how the scoring guide was used to score the responses.

Sample response that earned a score of 3

As a teacher who is trying to get parents to play a more active role in participating in literacy activities, I would encourage parents though a newsletter and a reading night. My newsletter would cite important things we are doing as a class to promote literacy. I would talk about the benefits of reading through research. I would enlighten parents on fun and exciting books that they should read to their children. I would also include a form that the parent fills out detailing how much time the child spends reading every day and what they read. My reading night will be a fun night for parents and students to read together at school. I will start by reading a book to everyone, then parents and students will be able to read books from the classroom together. This shows parents what they need to do with their child, exposes them to children literature that they may not have seen, and show them that I feel that this is so important that I would use my personal time to host the event.

In order to help parents to take a more active role, I would offer the following two suggestions. First read to/with your child every night. This is so simple, yet so important. Children become better readers everytime they read. Second, I would tell parents to immerse their child in a print rich environment. They need to fill their house with books, magazines, posters, letters, etc. Students need to see that reading is everywhere and that it is fun. Students may be more apt to read from a magazine, rather than a book.

By communicating and offering advice to parents, I feel that I can help them play a more active role in literacy.

Scoring Commentary

Both parts of the exercise are responded to fully and accurately.

Two effective forms of communication are described in detail: a newsletter and a reading night.

Two ways are listed in which parents can take a proactive role in helping their children develop an appreciation of literature: reading to/with their child and immersing their child in a print-rich environment.

The response demonstrates a strong knowledge of subject matter relevant to the question.

There is extensive information concerning the forms of communication and rationales for the selection.

The response is insightful, developmentally appropriate, and substantive.

The newsletter offers information to parents, reading together is developmentally appropriate, and the suggestion to immerse their child in a print-rich environment is substantive.

The suggestions are connected, effective, and developmentally appropriate.

All of the suggestions are related to developing an appreciation of literature in children. They are effective and developmentally appropriate for first-grade students.

Sample Responses to Question 62, continued

Sample response that earned a score of 2

> Parent support is critical for a student's success in reading. In order to ensure parent involvement I would implement two programs. First, to maintain open communication with parents I would see home a weekly reading log to get an idea of the amount of time the parent is reading to or with the child. In addition to the reading log, I would send home a book bag each week to ensure that both the parent & the student are exposed to developmentally appropriate literature. On a monthly basis, I would conduct a nightly literature circle with parents & students to discuss the literature read over the past month. Again, the parents will gain a more active role and communication lines with remain open.

Scoring Commentary

Some parts of the question are not answered appropriately.

Two forms of communication are described: a weekly reading log and a book bag. They are not described in detail, and no explanation is provided about how these forms of communication will help parents understand the importance of an appreciation of literature.

Only one way is listed in which parents can take a proactive role in helping their children develop an appreciation of literature: a literature circle to be held one night a month. The question clearly asks for *two* ways.

The response may demonstrate only superficial knowledge of subject matter relevant to the question.

No explanation is included concerning how a weekly reading log will help parents understand the importance of developing their child's appreciation of literature. Reference to the fact that sending a book bag each week will "ensure that both the parent and the student are exposed to developmentally appropriate literature" reflects a superficial understanding of the value of daily reading to reinforce literacy concepts. The literature circle, which will be held on a monthly basis, is a valuable suggestion that would be more meaningful with a full explanation of what the evening would involve and a rationale for the activities.

Sample response that earned a score of 1

> The two types of communication I would use is oral and body movement. I would in a loving but respectful manner which allows the parent to feel more comfortable. I would also speak in such a way as to convey that I am very knowledgeable on the subject. I need to also be very persuasive. My body language would be positioned in such a way as to make the parents comfortable. I would use good posture, hold my head up, and speak clearly.
>
> Some suggestions I would make is to read aloud with them daily. Also I would tell them to also engage in learning and show the child that literature can be wonderful.

Scoring Commentary

Most parts of the question are not answered adequately.

The two types of communication mentioned (oral and body movement) are inappropriate responses for the question since they will not help parents understand the importance of developing their child's appreciation of literature.

The suggestion to read aloud on a daily basis is appropriate for the parents to take a proactive role in helping their children develop an appreciation of literature, but the second suggestion—to "engage in learning and show the child that literature can be wonderful"—is too vague.

The response demonstrates weak understanding of the subject matter.

The response fails to describe in detail two effective forms of communication that could be used to help parents understand the importance of an appreciation of literature and thus demonstrates a weak understanding of literacy concepts.

The description is sketchy, inappropriate, or trivial.

The only valid suggestion, to read aloud on a daily basis, is not fully developed. The other suggestions are inappropriate or invalid.

The explanation is ineffective, loosely connected, partial, or missing.

The explanation that is provided in Part A concerning the two types of communication is ineffective since the forms of communication that have been selected (oral and body movement) will not achieve the goal of helping parents understand the importance of an appreciation of literature. Part B is missing an explanation that would help the reader to understand the rationale that would support the suggestions chosen.

Question 63

> You are planning an integrated unit on weather for the diverse learners in your kindergarten class.
>
> **Part A:** Describe ONE developmentally appropriate, weather-related activity that integrates the following disciplines:
>
> - science
> - language arts
> - math
>
> **Part B:** Discuss the conceptual understanding that the activity will address in each content area.

The same 0–3 scoring guide used for Question 61 is applied to each part of this question.

We will now look at three samples and see how the scoring guide was used to score the responses.

Sample Responses to Question 63, continued

Sample response that earned a score of 3

Science - 1 Our kindergarteners can play little weather forcasters. The students can do this with sunny, rainy, and cloudy days. The students can look outside to see if they see any of these elements, and predict what the rest of the day will be like. Students can also grow plants. The children will decide what type of weather makes plants grow best. Have students create their own tornado in a bottle. For the visual & hands-on student this activity will really nail home this idea. While discussing weather and the types of things included in weather - the topic of tornado can be brought up. Using soda bottles, water, sparkles and a connector. Students can cause the water to spin and this will demonstrate what happens to the air mixed with rain and the sparkles can represent debre - such as buildings people & houses. Language Arts -- 2 The students can draw what their family does when it is sunny outside and when it is rainy outside. They can dictate a sentence to go with the picture and the teacher can write it down. Students also can decide where are the best places to go in the community on rainy days and sunny days and draw pictures of the places that the teacher can label. Math -- 3 Have students chart the local weather - first by predicting the days (Forecast) and then study the weather for a period of time. Later have them reflect on the data they have collected - where their predicts correct - why or why not. Finally, have the class graph their findings & discuss what happened over that period of time.

Scoring Commentary

All parts of the exercise are responded to fully and accurately.

One developmentally appropriate weather-related activity is described (forecasting the weather, drawing activities for the weather types, and charting the weather), and the overall activity integrates science, language arts, and math. The response addresses the conceptual understanding that the activity will address for each discipline.

The response demonstrates a strong knowledge of subject matter relevant to the question.

The response demonstrates a strong knowledge of science, language arts, and math, as well as how to integrate the three disciplines.

The response is insightful, developmentally appropriate, and substantive.

The response is developmentally appropriate and incorporates hands-on activities (making a tornado, drawing activities related to various weather types, constructing a weather graph). The activities suggested are appropriate for kindergarten students and will help them to develop concepts in science, language arts, and mathematics.

The suggestions are connected, effective, and developmentally appropriate.

The suggestions are connected and effective. The children will be interested in the activities and will find them to be relevant to their experiences. The knowledge that the children will acquire from completing the activities will be relevant to prior experiences and therefore will be more comprehensible for them.

Sample response that earned a score of 2

Science - I would have the student's go outside and collect leaves from the trees in different areas around the school. We could then talk about the leaves and determine what season it is. I would explain that leaves fall from trees in the fall and why, why trees don't have leaves in the winter, and why trees grow leaves in the spring. Language arts -- the students could talk about what the weather and the leaves are like where they live or talk about other places they have visited and the weather and the leaves there. They could even talk about how different weather makes them feel. They could draw pictures and write words to describe the weather and the leaves.

Scoring Commentary

Some parts of the question are not answered appropriately.

Only two of the disciplines are mentioned (science and language arts), and the discussion of the conceptual understanding that the activity will address in each content area is limited. As a result, some parts of the question are not answered appropriately. The third discipline (mathematics) should be included, and the explanation concerning the activity choice should be more fully developed.

The response may demonstrate only superficial knowledge of subject matter relevant to the question.

The response demonstrates only superficial knowledge of science, language arts, and math and how to integrate these three disciplines within one science-related activity. A stronger understanding of science would be reflected in an activity that would be interdisciplinary and developmentally appropriate.

The response is only somewhat developmentally appropriate.

The activity involves a discussion of leaves that is only somewhat developmentally appropriate for kindergarten students ("I would explain that leaves fall from trees in the fall and why, why trees don't have leaves in the winter, and why trees grow leaves in the spring"). Kindergarten students may not be developmentally ready to fully grasp the concept of why trees shed leaves in fall and grow new leaves in spring. Another, more basic, concept would be more appropriate.

The explanation is appropriate, but not as closely connected as in a score of 3.

A more fully developed explanation would clarify the rationale for choosing this science activity to integrate different disciplines. The rationale that is provided is limited and does not offer insight concerning the activity selection or its benefits.

Sample Responses to Question 63, continued

Sample response that earned a score of 1

> First I would explain to students that the weather is different in different areas. That just because it is nice here it could raining some place else. I would show them picture books of different places & have them look at them on a map, to help explain the different weather.
>
> Have students watch the news a look at the different patterns then have them design their "ideal" weather for one week.

Scoring Commentary

Most parts of the question are not answered adequately.

Part A requires the description of one developmentally appropriate, weather-related activity that integrates the disciplines of science, language arts, and math, but no specific activity is presented and there is no mention of the three disciplines that should be considered. Part B asks for the conceptual understanding that the activity will address in each content area, but no explanation is provided.

The response demonstrates weak understanding of the subject matter.

The response demonstrates a weak understanding of science and how to integrate it with language arts and mathematics. The information presented involves the teacher telling the students information ("First I would explain to students that the weather is different in different areas. That just because it is nice here it could raining some place else"), or showing them pictures ("I would show them picture books of different places & have them look at them on a map, to help explain the different weather"), or watching television ("Have students watch the news a look at the different patterns then have them design their 'ideal' weather for one week"). None of the suggestions encourages the students to become actively involved in the learning process. For students at the kindergarten level, it is crucial that scientific learning be hands-on in order for them be able to comprehend the information.

The description is sketchy, inappropriate, or trivial.

The description is sketchy, inappropriate, and trivial. The description of the activity does not fully explain the role that the children will play and how their participation will help them to comprehend the concepts.

The explanation is ineffective, loosely connected, partial, or missing.

The explanation is ineffective because it does not explain the choice for the science activity or how the activity will be used to foster skills in other discipline areas (language arts and mathematics). A well-developed explanation would support the selection of the activity and reflect an understanding of the principles of learning and child development.

Question 64

STUDENT ASSIGNMENT: Add these problems. Show your work.

$34 + 9 =$ $67 + 18 =$ $35 + 17 =$

$$\begin{array}{r} 34 \\ +\ 9 \\ \hline 313 \end{array} \qquad \begin{array}{r} 67 \\ +18 \\ \hline 715 \end{array} \qquad \begin{array}{r} 35 \\ +17 \\ \hline 412 \end{array}$$

Part A: The children in a second-grade class are completing a math assignment. Above is a sample of a student's work. Discuss TWO aspects of mathematics development that are evident in the student's work.

Part B: Based on the mathematics skills identified in Part A, describe TWO developmentally appropriate instructional strategies you might use to advance this child's mathematical skills.

The same 0–3 scoring guide used for Question 61 is applied to each part of this question.

We will now look at three samples and see how the scoring guide was used to score the responses.

Sample response that earned a score of 3

One strength in this child's work is that he she writes the math problem correctly, by keeping the tens place in line with the tens place and the ones place in line with the one's place. Another strength is that the child knows that $4 + 9 = 13$, $3 + 0 = 3$, $7 + 8 = 15$, $6 + 1 = 7$, $3 + 1 = 4$, and $5 + 7 = 12$, The child just did not know how to carry over and borrow numbers.

In order to advance this child's understanding I would have them use manipulative base 10 rods and units to add the numbers. First I would go back and have the child add numbers like $33 + 24$ where the answer is a single digit. The child would do this with the base 10 rods and units. We would talk about place value (in $33 + 24$ we end up with 5 tens and 7 ones) and we would look at the problems with the rods and units. Then we would start doing problems like $34 + 9$ but first with the rods and units. This would make the problems visual so they will see that $34 + 9 = 43$ $67 + 18 = 85$ and $35 + 17 = 52$. I think the only problem here is not knowing how to borrow and carry over numbers—The knowledge of adding is there.

Scoring Commentary

All parts of the exercise are responded to fully and accurately.

Part A discusses two aspects of mathematics development that are evident in the student's work: lining up numbers correctly to maintain place value and knowledge of basic addition facts.

Sample Responses to Question 64, continued

Part B describes two developmentally appropriate instructional strategies used to advance the child's mathematical skills: base 10 rods and units, and beginning with problems that do not require regrouping before advancing to more complex problems that require regrouping.

The response demonstrates a strong knowledge of subject matter relevant to the question.

The response demonstrates a strong knowledge of mathematics. The student's strengths are identified and the test taker recognizes that the student has a good understanding of skills involved in computation. The instructional strategies are presented and offer a logical sequence for instruction that will help the student understand basic concepts before advancing to more complex concepts.

The response is insightful, developmentally appropriate, and substantive.

It is developmentally appropriate to provide a second-grade student with manipulatives that will provide concrete representation for abstract concepts. It is also developmentally appropriate to begin with basic concepts before advancing to more complex ones.

The suggestions are connected, effective, and developmentally appropriate.

The suggestions are connected, effective, and developmentally appropriate. The strengths that are identified refer to an understanding of place value and basic addition facts. The strategies build on these identified skills by focusing on place value in the use of manipulatives and advancing from two-digit addition without regrouping to two-digit addition with regrouping.

Sample response that earned a score of 2

Part A

Two areas of strength:

1. can add single column (the ones column)

2. knows that adding two numbers results in a larger number than each of the numbers.

Part B

One way I would try to help this child would be to have him/her concentrate on one column of numbers at a time by covering the rest. This way, the child could assimilate adding two numbers vertically can be advanced to more than just single-digit numbers, but that the procedure is pretty much the same.

Scoring Commentary

Some parts of the question are not answered appropriately.

Two aspects of mathematics development that are evident in the student's work are identified: ability to add single-column digits and knowledge that adding two numbers results in a larger number than either of the original numbers. Part A is answered appropriately.

Part B is supposed to describe TWO developmentally appropriate instructional strategies to advance the child's mathematical skills, but only one strategy is provided (to have the child concentrate on one column of numbers at a time by covering the rest). A second strategy is necessary to attain a score of 3.

The response may demonstrate only superficial knowledge of subject matter relevant to the question.

It is not clear from the response how having the student "concentrate on one column of numbers at a time by covering the rest" would help the student to advance to two-digit addition that requires regrouping. A more complete response would reflect a deeper understanding of the subject matter—in this case, mathematical skills involving two-digit addition with regrouping.

The response is only somewhat developmentally appropriate.

Second grade children learn best when using manipulatives, but the response focuses on the abstract use of numbers. A more developmentally appropriate response would focus on providing the child with a concrete understanding of this abstract concept.

The explanation is appropriate, but not as closely connected as in a score of 3.

The child's strengths are described as "can add single column (the ones column)" and "knows that adding two numbers results in a larger number than each of the numbers," but no additional explanation is provided to support this statement. The question clearly states "describe," yet the response is merely a statement, not a description of the child's mathematical development. A better-developed explanation would clarify the basic statement.

Part B should also be developed to explain how focusing on one column at a time will help the child to understand two-digit addition with regrouping. A second explanation should also be included to explain another instructional strategy that would be appropriate for this student.

Sample response that earned a score of 1

> Just by looking at the student's work w/out real examination, I can see that the student is a problem-solver and works things out. He/She also works problems out in his/her head.
>
> I would encourage this student to work problems out in his/her head, but to also work out problems on the paper. Utilizing both these ways will assist the student with the math problems.

Sample Responses to Question 64, continued

Scoring Commentary

Most parts of the question are not answered adequately.

For Part A, the first strength ("that the student is a problem-solver") is very vague, while the second strength ("he/she also works problems out in his/her head") is not supported by the student's work sample. Most of Part A would not be considered adequate.

Part B appears to recommend two strategies ("to work problems out in his/her head, but to also work out problems on the paper") but does not describe how to apply these strategies. The strategies also reflect what was done by the student in the work sample and do not add additional information concerning the advancement of the student's mathematical skills. Most of Part B would not be considered adequate.

The response demonstrates weak understanding of the subject matter.

The response fails to identify valid strengths of the student and appropriate strategies that would help the student and therefore reflects a weak understanding of the subject matter. A stronger understanding of mathematical skills and instructional strategies would result in an accurate analysis of the student's strengths and of how to advance the student's mathematical skills.

The description is sketchy, inappropriate, or trivial.

The descriptions in both Parts A and B are sketchy, inappropriate, and trivial. Part A indicates aspects of mathematics development ("that the student is a problem-solver and…works problems out in his/her head") that are not supported by the student's work sample. Part B repeats some of Part A ("encourage this student to work problems out in his/her head") and adds a strategy that is not well-developed ("work out problems on the paper"). More information is necessary for both parts.

The explanation is ineffective, loosely connected, partial, or missing.

No explanation is provided for either Part A or Part B. Aspects of mathematics development are stated ("that the student is a problem-solver and…works problems out in his/her head") and strategies are presented ("encourage this student to work problems out in his/her head, but to also work out problems on the paper") but neither part is explained. Explanations would clarify the information presented and the rationale for its selection.

Question 65

You are the preschool teacher of 4-year-old Roberta. One of Roberta's parents comes to pick her up after school and drive her home. This is the first time you have observed the parent with slurred speech and clumsy movements. You suspect that the parent has been drinking.

Part A: Based on practice that is ethical as well as professionally and legally prudent, what are your responsibilities to Roberta and her family as a teacher?

Part B: List THREE resources that you could use to help you to learn how best to handle the issues specific to this situation. Describe the information each resource could provide.

The same 0–3 scoring guide used for Question 61 is applied to each part of this question.

We will now look at three samples and see how the scoring guide was used to score the responses.

Sample response that earned a score of 3

According to the NAEYC Code of Ethics my first and primary concern is the safety of the child. Rather than rush to judge there maybe other reasons for this parent's slurred speech. I would quietly talk with the parent and try to assess the situation, by asking them if they would like to see what the child worked on today. My reason for doing this is to keep the child out of the parent's car.

I would ask a colleague to get the principal/director and tell her of my suspicions. If the nurse or social worker is avaible, I would ask their help in intervening in this situation. I would also try and contact another adult listed on the child's pick-up list to come and pick up the child/parent. I would also need to document this situation just in case this issue arose once again.

Scoring Commentary

All parts of the exercise are responded to fully and accurately.

The response is fully developed and accurate. Part A refers to the NAEYC Code of Ethics and the teacher's responsibility for the safety of the child. Part B lists three resources (principal/director, nurse or social worker, another adult on the child's pick-up list) to help the teacher learn how best to handle the issues specific to this situation.

The response demonstrates a strong knowledge of subject matter relevant to the question.

The response demonstrates a strong knowledge of ethical and legal implications for the scenario described. It also reflects knowledge of resources that would be available for the teacher in dealing with the situation. The resources have been identified and are appropriate for helping the child, the parent, and the teacher resolve the situation.

Sample Responses to Question 65, continued

The response is insightful, developmentally appropriate, and substantive.

The response is highly insightful, allowing for a variety of causes for slurred speech, rather than assuming that alcohol is the only option. The teacher's response reflects actions that are thoughtful and involve a consideration of the child's safety as well as a respectful approach toward the child's parent. This response is developmentally appropriate for a situation that involves a 4-year-old child.

The suggestions are connected, effective, and developmentally appropriate.

All of the suggestions are connected, effective, and developmentally appropriate. They reflect a careful consideration of the situation and a plan to resolve the problem effectively while maintaining the safety of both the child and the parent.

Sample response that earned a score of 2

I would ask the parent to come into the office to talk in private then I would see if there is anyone else who could come to pick up the such as the other parent. If the parent declines to provide another person to come get the child then I would tell that person that I cannot allow them to take the child under these conditions. I would then show them the policy book which will have this listed as one of the reasons to not allow the child to leave with an individual who has been suspected of drinking. Then I would make contact with the local DHS office to report the case so that if it occurs again they will be aware of the situation and for them to follow up with the family and offer other resources to help the parent. I would also have a local number for the parent to call if they want to get help with a drinking problem. Then I would make contact with the other parent to come pick up the child. If this parent is unable to come then I would have them authorize someone to come pick up the child. Also, I would go over the policy with this parent so they will be aware of the reason the child was not able to leave with a parent that has been drinking.

Scoring Commentary

Some parts of the question are not answered appropriately.

Part A is not fully developed and therefore not answered appropriately. There is no clear reference to the teacher's responsibilities to Roberta and her family. There is also an assumption that the slurred speech and clumsy movements are related to the single cause of drinking, with no mention of possible alternative causes.

The response may demonstrate only superficial knowledge of subject matter relevant to the question.

Part A does not reflect knowledge of the ethical and legal responsibilities of a teacher. There is also an assumption that a policy book will clearly state all the factors involved in this scenario and that the parent will refer to the policy book and accept the guidelines of the school. Part B refers to valid resources for long-term intervention ("the local DHS office" and "a local number for the parent to call if they want to get help with a drinking problem"), but only one contact for immediate assistance ("the other parent to come pick up the child" or "have them authorize someone to come pick up the child"). Stronger knowledge of this area would be reflected in a more appropriate response.

The response is only somewhat developmentally appropriate.

The response is somewhat developmentally appropriate, in that the teacher is intervening to ensure the safety of the child; however, it would be more developmentally appropriate if Part A referred specifically to the teacher's responsibilities and if Part B provided resources who would be able to assist the child as well as the parent.

The explanation is appropriate, but not as closely connected as in a score of 3.

Part A is not fully developed, and a fuller explanation would have raised the score for this response. More information needs to be provided to determine whether the teacher fully understands her responsibilities based on practice that is ethical as well as professionally and legally prudent. Part B provides some explanations, but a stronger rationale for the selection of the resources would have strengthened this response overall.

Sample response that earned a score of 1

Part A: I would begin by approaching the parent & ask her how thiongs are going etc...all in a pleasant, non-suspecting way. I will be trying to stall time at first but then I would ask her to come & meet with one so that I could talk with her about her daughter. I do not wan her to think that I know she has been drinking.

Scoring Commentary

Most parts of the question are not answered adequately.

Part A begins appropriately, but the information provided is not sufficient to determine whether the teacher fully understands a teacher's responsibilities to Roberta and her family. Initiating a conversation with the parent is a valid strategy to use in this situation, but this strategy is not developed enough to be considered adequate.

No response is provided for Part B.

The response demonstrates weak understanding of the subject matter.

The information that is provided demonstrates a weak understanding of how to deal with ethical and legal situations. Part A is not fully developed and Part B is missing.

The description is sketchy, inappropriate, or trivial.

The description provided in Part A is sketchy and undeveloped. While "stall[ing for] time" is a good primary step to take in dealing with this scenario, the description needs to be developed and supported by subsequent actions in order to be considered appropriate. Part B is missing and is therefore inappropriate.

Sample Responses to Question 65, continued

The explanation is ineffective, loosely connected, partial, or missing.

The explanation for Part A is ineffective and partial, since only the initial steps are presented and the explanation is not developed. More information concerning the teacher's responsibilities needs to be included. Part B is missing, with no explanation provided.

Question 66

> Dylan is a child in your second-grade class who has a physical handicap that requires the use of a wheelchair.
>
> **Part A:**   Describe TWO appropriate adaptations or accommodations that would help Dylan continue to learn.
>
> **Part B:**   Explain how each adaptation or accommodation described in Part A could benefit Dylan.

The same 0–3 scoring guide used for Question 61 is applied to each part of this question.

We will now look at three samples and see how the scoring guide was used to score the responses.

Sample response that earned a score of 3

If I were a second grade teacher with a student in a wheelchair I would adapt my classroom so that anything on the walls or shelves would be reachable to that child. For instance if I had a special board where the children were to get passes to leave the room I would make sure that board was in the armspan of the special needs student. Being able to reach items that are used in the classroom will benefit the child so they can get the supplies needed for a lesson or activity. It will aid in the student's independence because they wont have to rely on others to reach items for them. Another way I would accomodate this student would be to make sure any aisles between desks or any space in the room is big enough for the child's wheelchair to fit through. This way the child can move about the room as freely as any other student. It will benefit the student to be able to get to any part of the classroom without difficulty. The student will know that they can go anywhere that other children are able to go in the classroom. Again it will help them to be more independent.

Scoring Commentary

All parts of the exercise are responded to fully and accurately.

Both Parts A and B are responded to fully and accurately. Part A describes two appropriate adaptations or accommodations that would help Dylan continue to learn: "anything on the walls or shelves would be reachable" and "any aisles between desks or any space in the room is big enough for the child's wheelchair to fit through."

The explanations presented in Part B are fully developed and reflect an understanding of the child's need for independence, as well as his need for access to materials.

The response demonstrates a strong knowledge of subject matter relevant to the question.

The response reflects a strong knowledge of how to modify a classroom environment to accommodate the needs of an individual child. The accommodations allow the child to participate fully in class activities and do not interfere with the needs and activities of his classmates.

The response is insightful, developmentally appropriate, and substantive.

The response is insightful, commenting that placing materials at an appropriate level "will aid in the student's independence because they won't have to rely on others to reach items for them," and that with sufficient space in the classroom "the child can move about the room as freely as any other student." This response is developmentally appropriate since students in second grade enjoy being independent and receiving treatment that is equivalent to that of their peers.

The suggestions are connected, effective, and developmentally appropriate.

The suggestions are connected, effective, and developmentally appropriate. They will serve to help Dylan as he continues to learn and will benefit all of the students in the classroom. The suggestions consider the individual needs of Dylan as well as his role as a student in a class and effectively meet the needs of all the children.

Sample response that earned a score of 2

> In accomodating a child in a wheelchair it takes careful planning and consideration. Accomodations would have to begin at a basic level in providing a desk wide enough for a wheelchair to fit under. The desks would need to be arranged in a pattern conducive to movement freely around the classroom. The student needs to feel included and accepted on all levels.
>
> A child will feel more capable and self-sufficient if they can freely acess the classroom in the same manner as other class mates. Inclusion is not complete until all students are equally included. Many other adaptations in the classroom would need to occur in order for the child to feel sucess.

Scoring Commentary

Some parts of the question are not answered appropriately.

Some parts of the question are not answered appropriately, in that both Part A and Part B should be more developed. The suggestions for Part A (to provide a desk wide enough for a wheelchair to fit under and to arrange the desks in a pattern conducive to movement freely around the classroom) are appropriate; however, the explanation in Part B does not directly refer back to these suggestions to elaborate how the accommodations would benefit Dylan.

Sample Responses to Question 66, continued

The response may demonstrate only superficial knowledge of subject matter relevant to the question.

The undeveloped explanation in Part B demonstrates only superficial knowledge of how to modify a classroom to accommodate the needs of an individual child. The statement that "a child will feel more capable and self-sufficient if they can freely access the classroom" does not fully support the accommodations that were made. Additional information would be necessary to reflect a strong knowledge of this area.

The response is only somewhat developmentally appropriate.

The response is somewhat developmentally appropriate in that the accommodations would make the student more independent; however, second grade students like to be just like their peers, and placing a student at a bigger desk may make the child feel different from his classmates. A better developed explanation might have clarified how this accommodation would occur to ensure that the child's needs are met while maintaining his role as a second grade student.

The explanation is appropriate, but not as closely connected as in a score of 3.

The explanation for Part B should be more developed to explain how the accommodations could benefit Dylan. A clearer explanation in Part B would clarify the choices for accommodations that are presented in Part A, resulting in an overall response that is closer to a score of 3.

Sample response that earned a score of 1

Part A - The arrangement of the room would make a huge difference in this child's life. You should have the room prearranged for his convience. This would also help with the other students wondering why we arranged the room special for him. The rules of the classroom should be stressed to be courtious and kind to everyone.

Part B - The arrangement of the room would be beneficial because the child would not have to bump into things when moving around in the room. The rules should prevent anyone being unkind to the student or anyone else.

Scoring Commentary

Most parts of the question are not answered adequately.

Part A does not describe two appropriate adaptations or accommodations that would help Dylan continue to learn. The response refers to the arrangement of the room but does not specifically describe the arrangement. Rules of the classroom are mentioned, but no other accommodation is provided; therefore, Part A is not answered adequately.

Part B states that "the arrangement of the room would be beneficial because the child would not have to bump into things when moving around in the room" but does not explain how this accommodation could benefit Dylan. Part B is not answered adequately.

The response demonstrates weak understanding of the subject matter.

The response demonstrates weak understanding of how to modify a classroom to accommodate the needs of an individual student. Additional information concerning the accommodations and explanations concerning these accommodations would be necessary to reflect a strong understanding of this area.

The description is sketchy, inappropriate, or trivial.

The description is sketchy in that additional information would be needed to clarify the accommodations and the rationale. A description concerning what the arrangement of the room would involve, along with a second accommodation, would strengthen Part A.

Part B would be enhanced by an explanation about how the specific arrangement could benefit Dylan. A second explanation should also be included about an additional accommodation.

The explanation is ineffective, loosely connected, partial, or missing.

The explanation is ineffective and loosely connected, failing to explain the recommended accommodation fully. A more effective explanation would strengthen Part A and would clarify the choice of accommodations. A second explanation is necessary to develop the second recommended accommodation since it is unclear whether the second accommodation ("The rules of the classroom should be stressed") is undeveloped, inappropriate, or missing. Additional information in the form of an explanation would clarify the response.

Chapter 9
Are You Ready? Last-Minute Tips

▶ ▶ ▶ ▶ ▶ ▶ ▶ ▶ ▶ ▶ ▶

Checklist

Complete this checklist to determine whether you're ready to take the test.

❏ Do you know the testing requirements for your field in the state(s) where you plan to teach?

❏ Have you followed all of the test registration procedures?

❏ Do you know the topics covered in each test you plan to take?

❏ Have you reviewed any textbooks, class notes, musical pieces, and course readings related to the topics covered?

❏ Do you know how long the test will take and the number of questions it contains? Have you considered how you will pace your work?

❏ Are you familiar with the test directions and the types of questions in the test?

❏ Are you familiar with the recommended test-taking strategies and tips?

❏ Have you worked through the practice test questions at a pace similar to that of an actual test?

❏ If you are repeating a Praxis Series™ assessment, have you analyzed your previous score report to determine areas where additional study and test preparation could be useful?

The Day of the Test

You should end your review a day or two before the actual test date. The day of the test you should

- Be well rested

- Take photo identification with you

- Take a supply of well-sharpened #2 pencils (at least three) if you are taking a multiple-choice test

- Take blue or black ink pens if you are taking a constructed-response test

- Take your admission ticket, letter of authorization, mailgram or telegram with you

- Eat before you take the test to keep your energy level up

- Wear layered clothing; room temperature may vary

- Be prepared to stand in line to check in or to wait while other test takers are being checked in

You can't control the testing situation, but you can control yourself. Stay calm. The supervisors are well trained and make every effort to provide uniform testing conditions, but don't let it bother you if the test doesn't start exactly on time. You will have the full amount of time once it does start.

Think of preparing for this test as training for an athletic event. Once you've trained, prepared, and rested, give it everything you've got. Good luck.

Appendix A
Study Plan Sheet

▶ ▶ ▶ ▶ ▶ ▶ ▶ ▶ ▶ ▶ ▶ ▶

Study Plan Sheet

See chapter 1 for suggestions about using this Study Plan Sheet.

STUDY PLAN						
Content covered on test	How well do I know the content?	What material do I have for studying this content?	What material do I need for studying this content?	Where could I find the materials I need?	Dates planned for study of content	Dates completed

Appendix B
For More Information

▶ ▶ ▶ ▶ ▶ ▶ ▶ ▶ ▶ ▶ ▶ ▶

ETS offers additional information to assist you in preparing for The Praxis Series Assessments. *Tests at a Glance* material and the *Registration Bulletin* are both available without charge (see below to order). You can also obtain more information from our Web site: www.ets.org/praxis

General Inquires

Phone: 609-771-7395 (Monday-Friday, 8:00 A.M. to 8:00 P.M., Eastern time)

Fax: 609-771-7906

Extended Time

If you have a learning disability or if English is not your primary language, you can apply to be given more time to take your test. The *Registration Bulletin* tells you how you can qualify for extended time.

Disability Services

Phone: 609-771-7780

Fax: 609-771-7906

TTY (for deaf or hard-of-hearing callers): 609-771-7714

Mailing Address

The Praxis Series™
Educational Testing Service
P.O. Box 6051
Princeton, NJ 08541-6051

Overnight Delivery Address

The Praxis Series™
Educational Testing Service
Distribution Center
225 Phillips Blvd.
P.O. Box 77435
Ewing, NJ 08628-7435